Introduction

Light & Healthy Microwave Cooking is more than another cookbook. It is an interesting, practical guide for incorporating healthy eating into your lifestyle, a unique book that offers the facts about good nutrition and provides tips for making the facts reality in your life. The authors, a home economist and a registered dietitian, have years of experience in teaching nutrition and microwave cooking. In *Light & Healthy Microwave Cooking*, they've teamed up to share their knowledge. The first chapter presents the guidelines for a healthful diet as developed by top scientists at the U.S. Department of Agriculture and the U.S. Department of Health, Education and Welfare. In the following pages, you'll learn how to put those guidelines into practice. Every chapter combines explicit hints, useful notes on the latest in nutrition information—and great recipes.

Light & Healthy Microwave Cooking offers healthful versions of dozens of traditional favorites: Breakfast Home Fries, Skinny Shrimp Scampi, Chicken Cordon Bleu, Chocolate Mousse and Creamy Cheesecake. Every dish is delicious and nutritious. Many are low in fat, sugar and salt and high in fiber and calcium. Unique to this microwave cookbook is the bar-chart nutritional analysis accompanying every recipe. An easy-to-read chart displays each recipe's total calories and the relative caloric distribution of carbohydrates, protein and fats.

Who is this book for? *Light & Healthy Microwave Cooking* has something for everybody. Using these recipes, even individuals with specific dietary restrictions can dine deliciously with no feelings of deprivation. In every page of this book, the authors show that healthful eating can easily be an everyday experience. Eating right is the best insurance policy for excellent health—and with the help of the microwave, eating right has never been simpler!

The Microwave is a Natural

Microwave cooking is a natural part of a healthy lifestyle. Whether you're counting calories, cutting down on sugar or salt or just trying to maintain a healthful diet, you'll find that the microwave makes meal preparation a breeze. Microwaved foods look good and taste great—and they're often more nutritious than their conventionally-cooked counterparts. Microwaved fruits and vegetables require very little water for cooking, so vitamins are retained in the food instead of boiling away in the cooking liquid. Microwaving means beautiful bright colors, too; a gorgeous array of tender-crisp microwaved vegetables is always a winner at parties. Another microwave bonus is better texture. Quick microwaving leaves foods juicy, tender, and more moist than if cooked by conventional methods.

What if you're on a special diet—low-salt, low-sugar or low-calorie? The microwave can be a big help here. Because microwaving enhances flavors of natural sugar and salt in foods, you may not even be tempted to reach for the salt shaker or the sugar bowl. And, microwaving often cuts calories: little or no fat is needed as foods cook in their own moisture and don't tend to stick to the dish. If you microwave your meals, the calories you *didn't* use for fat can be "spent" on another food—without exceeding your daily calorie limit.

Light & Healthy
MICROWAVE COOKING

Janet Emal

Janet Emal received a degree in Home Economics from California State University in Sacramento, California. With an extensive background in food and nutrition, she now teaches classes in weight control, low-calorie gourmet cooking and microwave cooking at Phoenix College.

As a free-lance home economist, Janet currently works with a bariatric physician, teaching his patients healthful, low-calorie microwave cooking, manages a local cooking school, lectures for community events and publishes a quarterly microwave newsletter, *SunWaves*.

Janet is co-author of another successful HPBook, *Kids Cook Microwave*. She resides in Phoenix, Arizona with her husband and two children. The family has enjoyed sampling many healthful meals along the way to *Light & Healthy Microwave Cooking*.

Elizabeth Taylor, R.D.

Elizabeth Taylor is a registered dietitian in private practice in Sacramento, California. As a nutrition consultant for Sacramento Endocrinogist, Liz specializes in designing diets to fit the individual medical needs and lifestyles of her patients. She also teaches weekly nutrition education classes. Before consulting with Sacramento Endocrinogist, Liz was the nutrition spokesperson for Sutter Community Hospital, where she developed care plans for pregnant, nursing and weight-control clients.

Liz has written numerous articles relating to diet and lifestyle for St. Joseph's Hospital and Medical Center, Phoenix, Arizona, lectures on a variety of diet and health topics and frequently appears on television and radio programs throughout California. She is a member of the California Dietetic Association and chairwoman of the Public Relations Committee of the Sacramento Dietetic Association.

She enjoys preparing nutritious microwave meals for her husband and two sons.

CONTENTS

Another Best-Selling Volume from HPBooks®

Publisher: Rick Bailey; Executive Editor: Randy Summerlin
Editorial Director: Elaine R. Woodard; Editors: Rebecca LaBrum, Patricia Aaron
Art Director: Don Burton; Book Design: Leslie Sinclair
Production Coordinator: Cindy J. Coatsworth; Typography: Michelle Carter
Director of Manufacturing: Anthony B. Narducci
Food Stylist: Susan Zechman; Photography: Cy DeCosse, Inc.

Published by HPBooks, A Division of HPBooks, Inc.
ISBN 0-89586-387-1
Library of Congress Catalog Card Number 86-82121
©1986 HPBooks, Inc.   Printed in the U.S.A.
1st Printing

Light and healthy party fare, featured on the following pages clockwise from upper right: Crunchy Vegetable
Rounds, page 141; Shrimp-Stuffed Sole on a bed of chopped spinach leaves, page 58; Marvelous Mushrooms, page 148; Peach Fondue surrounded with assorted fresh fruit for dipping, page 155

Using This Book

Light & Healthy Microwave Cooking is designed to assist in meeting diet-related health goals. In addition to covering traditional recipe categories such as meats, poultry and vegetables, we've devoted whole chapters to particular dietary goals—cooking with less salt, decreasing the sugar in desserts and making snacktime more nutritious. All in all, you'll find dozens of delicious, good-for-you recipes, all carefully tested, each analyzed for calorie count and amounts of key nutrients.

To ensure success with the recipes and get the most out of this book, use your oven correctly, use the right utensils—and learn to interpret the nutritional analysis following each recipe.

THE MICROWAVE OVEN

The recipes in this book were tested using several variable power microwave ovens between 650 and 700 watts. Much of the success of microwave cooking results from proper choice of power levels, so review the owner's manual carefully to understand the variable power percentages for your particular oven. The authors used the following percentages: 100% power *(HIGH)*, 70% power *(MEDIUM-HIGH)*, 50% power *(MEDIUM)*, and 30% power *(MEDIUM-LOW)*.

UTENSILS

Microwave-safe glass cooking utensils and suitable plastic microwave accessories *must* be used in the microwave oven. Consult the manufacturer's use and care manual or cookbook for information on which materials are safe for your oven. The authors used glass measures in many recipes; these are especially convenient for cooking as they have handles. Always use glass when cooking with foods high in sugar or fat, as melted fat and sugar can become hot enough to melt many plastic products.

For food with a short cooking time, you can often use paper plates as "cookware."

When a recipe tells you to cover tightly, use either a tight fitting lid or plastic wrap recommended for microwaving. A few recipes tell you to "cover with wax paper." Like plastic wrap, wax paper keeps food from drying out but it also lets some moisture evaporate. If you want to cover food to prevent spatters or absorb moisture or fat, use a paper towel.

NUTRITIONAL ANALYSIS

A unique feature of our book is the nutritional analysis following each recipe. All recipes have been analyzed for calories and three key nutrients: carbohydrates, proteins and fats. The low-salt chapter also includes an analysis of sodium content. The computerized analysis performed is based on information provided by the U.S. Department of Agriculture and several other handbooks.

As the following example illustrates, each recipe's bar chart displays the relative caloric distribution of carbohydrates, protein and fats per serving. The length of each bar is proportional to the total calories per serving; actual gram values of key nutrients are shown below each chart. In the low-salt chapter, sodium content is given along with servings, i.e.,—Makes 6 (96 mg sodium) servings—at the end of each recipe.

Carbohydrate 2.5 g	
Protein 9.3 g	
Fat 11.4 g	

Note: The authors have taken care to provide accurate nutritional analyses. The reader should be aware, however, that even when the recipes are followed exactly, variances in the nutritional values are likely due to variety, freshness and brand of ingredients used.

Note: The authors have taken care to provide accurate nutritional analyses. The reader should be aware, however, that even when the recipes are followed exactly, variances in the nutritional values are likely due to variety, freshness and brand of ingredients used.

Dietary Guidelines

In 1985, the U.S. Department of Agriculture and the U.S. Department of Health and Human Services updated their dietary guidelines (originally developed by USDA and HEW) in order to help Americans establish more healthful eating habits. These guidelines, intended for healthy people who do not have special dietary needs, are documented in the official manuscript **Nutrition and Your Health: Dietary Guidelines for Americans.** The seven basic guidelines (U.S. dietary goals) are:

- Eat a variety of foods.
- Maintain desirable body weight.
- Avoid too much fat, saturated fat and cholesterol.
- Eat foods with adequate starch and fiber.
- Avoid too much sugar.
- Avoid too much sodium.
- Drink alcoholic beverages in moderation.

The first two guidelines set up the basis of a good diet: *Eat a variety of foods in order to maintain desirable body weight.* The remaining five describe specific characteristics of healthy diets. In the next few pages, we expand on each of these guidelines in turn; throughout the book, you'll find recipes and tips for putting them into practice.

EAT A VARIETY OF FOODS

To function properly, the body needs more than 40 different nutrients, including protein, fat, carbohydrates, vitamins, minerals and water. Though most foods contain more than one nutrient, no single food provides all nutrients in the proper amount. The greater the variety of foods you eat, the less likely you are to suffer from a deficiency or excess of any one nutrient. To obtain all the nutrients your body requires, follow a daily diet that includes an assortment of foods from the five food groups:

- Vegetables and fruits
- Breads, cereals, legumes and grain products
- Dairy products: low-fat cheese, low-fat or nonfat milk and yogurt
- Meats, poultry, fish and eggs
- Fats, oils, sweets and alcohol

On page 14, you'll find more information on the five food groups and tips for working them into your diet.

MAINTAIN DESIRABLE BODY WEIGHT

Weight gain, loss or maintenance is determined by the balance of caloric intake and expenditure. If you consume more energy (calories) than you burn, you'll gain weight; if you burn more than you take in, you'll lose weight. To shed pounds, you must select lower-calorie foods, increase activity or—better still—do both.

Whether you're trying to reduce or just maintain your present weight, it's wise to follow certain rules. First, increase your awareness of food habits. Try writing down everything you eat each day; you may find that a few odd snacks here and there are adding up to more calories than you realized. Second, control portion sizes, by eating standard servings of each food (see page 14). And always keep the basic dietary goals in mind; avoid fats and fatty foods, eat more fruits and vegetables to increase fiber and cut down on alcohol and sweets.

CALORIES BURNED PER MINUTE OF EXERCISE

Activity	Calories Burned Per Minute*
Walking, 30 min/mile	3-4
Cycling, 12 min/mile	4-5
Bowling	4-5
Golfing	4-5
Volleyball	5-6
Walking, 12 min/mile	6-7
Cycling, 6 min/mile	6-7
Tennis, singles	7-8
Aerobic dancing	7-8
Swimming, moderate pace	8-10
Jogging, 12 min/mile	8-10
Racquetball	8-10
Basketball	10-11
Downhill skiing	10-11
Running, 8 min/mile	14-16
Cross-country skiing	14-16
Running, 6 min/mile	17-19

*These figures may vary according to weight and the intensity with which the exercise is performed.

Proper diet is only part of a complete health program. Regular exercise is the other half of the formula. Diet *plus* exercise add up to the most effective method of achieving weight loss and maintaining ideal body weight. Exercise burns calories, raises metabolism and builds muscle—and what's more, it just makes you feel good. If you're out of shape, start your exercise regimen slowly; research has shown that working off even as few as 200 calories a day can provide many health benefits. You can step up the pace of your workouts as your fitness increases. As the chart at left shows, exercises that require you to move your entire body result in the greatest caloric expenditure. Walking briskly for 30 minutes or more each day is one of the most effective forms of exercise.

Before you begin any exercise program, check with your doctor. And remember—whatever form of exercise you choose, don't overdo it. The goal is to train, not strain your body; exercise should be fun, not a grind.

AVOID TOO MUCH FAT . . .
SATURATED FAT AND CHOLESTEROL

We all need some fat in our diets. Of all the foods we eat, fat is the most concentrated source of energy. Gram for gram, it supplies over twice as many calories as protein or carbohydrates (nine calories per gram for fat, versus just four per gram for protein or carbohydrates). We also require fat for the synthesis and transport of hormones and vitamins A, D, E and K. What we don't need is too *much* fat; just one tablespoon daily satisfies the body's requirements.

Three types of fat are of most interest to nutritionists: saturated, polyunsaturated and monounsaturated. *Saturated fats,* solid at room temperature, occur in animal and some vegetable foods. Saturated animal fats are found in meats such as beef, lamb, pork and ham, in butter, cream and whole milk, and in cheeses made from cream or whole milk. Saturated vegetable fats include solid vegetable shortening, cocoa butter, coconut oil and palm oil. *Polyunsaturated fats,* liquid at room temperature, are primarily vegetable oils: safflower, sunflower, corn, soybean and cottonseed. Foods supplying *monounsaturated fats* include olives, olive oil, peanuts, peanut oil and avocados.

Because they elevate blood cholesterol levels, saturated fats in particular should be avoided. Manufactured naturally in the human liver and necessary in small amounts for good health, cholesterol may lead to an increased risk of heart disease if consumed in excess. Polyunsaturated fats—in contrast to saturated types—tend to lower blood cholesterol levels. Recent research indicates that the same is true of monounsaturated fats, long thought to have no effect on blood cholesterol levels.

The average American diet gets about 40% of its calories from fat. Nutritionists recommend cutting this amount to 30% or less: 10%—or preferably, less—from saturated fats, 10% or less from polyunsaturated fats, and the rest from monounsaturated fats. As for cholesterol, most doctors suggest a daily consumption of no more than 300 milligrams. Normal blood cholesterol levels range from 100 to 250 milligrams per 100 milliliters. Your doctor can tell you what your level should be. Even if your level falls within the normal range, keep track of how much cholesterol you eat each day—and try to keep it at or below the recommended amount.

EAT FOODS WITH ADEQUATE
STARCH AND FIBER

Starch often has a bad name among dieters; potatoes, bread and so on are generally considered fattening foods. But in fact, the complex carbohydrates found in vegetables, fruits, whole-grain breads, cereals and beans are our major source of energy. These same carbohydrate-rich foods also provide dietary fiber—the portion of a plant which cannot be broken down by our digestive enzymes. Fiber occurs in various forms in the foods we eat. Water-soluble fiber, such as pectins, mucilages and gums, is found in beans, oat bran, fruits and vegetables. Fiber not soluble in water—cellulose, lignin and hemicellulose—is contained in beans, vegetables and whole grains.

Fiber is not a nutrient, since the body cannot digest it. Nonetheless, it's essential for good health. Fiber helps keep the digestive track healthy and is thought to reduce the risk of certain cancers. Some fibers, chiefly pectins and gums, lower blood cholesterol levels, possibly by increasing cholesterol excretion. (Other types of fiber, such as that found in wheat bran, have no effect on cholesterol.) The stickiest fibers—the pectins and gums found in citrus fruits and vegetables—also help modulate levels of blood sugar.

There is no RDA established for fiber. Dietitians usually set 20 to 30 grams of dietary fiber per 1,000 calories as a standard amount for a high-fiber diet. If you need to increase your fiber consumption (and most Americans do), start by including more high-fiber foods in your daily meals. Don't add too much fiber too quickly. Excess dietary fiber can hinder the absorption of calcium, zinc and iron. As you increase your fiber intake, be sure to drink plenty of liquids.

To give you some ideas for increasing the fiber in your diet, check the table on page 10. It lists the fiber content of a number of everyday foods. Here are a few other ways to add fiber to your life:

- Start the day with high-fiber cereal.
- Eat whole fruit instead of drinking juice.
- Add corn, oat or wheat bran to breads, meat loaf, meatballs, casseroles and desserts.
- Cook with whole grains.

DIETARY FIBER CONTENT OF VARIOUS FOODS

Foods	Serving Size	Fiber Content (g)*
BREADS & CEREALS GROUP		
All-Bran or 100% Bran	3/4 cup	11.2
Bran Chex	1/2 cup	4.1
Shredded wheat	1 large biscuit	2.8
Grape-Nuts	3/4 cup	5.8
Grits, uncooked	1/4 cup dry	4.8
Oats, rolled	1/2 cup dry	4.5
Whole-wheat bread	1 slice	1.3
FRUIT GROUP		
Apple	1 medium	2.4
Pear	1 medium	4.4
Grapefruit	1/2 medium	1.0
Strawberries	1 cup	3.1
Orange	1 medium	1.8
Banana	1/2 medium	1.5
Peaches or Pears, canned	1/2 cup	1.3
VEGETABLES		
Corn, cooked	1/2 cup	4.7
Peas, cooked	1/2 cup	3.8
Carrot, raw	1/2 cup	2.8
Potato, baked	1 medium	3.8
Summer squash, uncooked	1/2 cup	2.0
Broccoli, cooked	3/4 cup	5.0
GRAINS & LEGUMES		
Lentils, cooked	1/2 cup	3.7
Rice, brown, cooked	1 cup	1.1
Rice, white, cooked	1 cup	0.4

*Based on Handbook of Clinical Dietetics, American Dietetics Association figures.

AVOID TOO MUCH SUGAR

Each day, the average American consumes about 500 low-nutrition calories from plain old sugar. This is not a healthy habit. Research shows that the more often sugar and high-sugar foods are eaten, the greater the risk of tooth decay. Studies also indicate that the consumption of refined sugars stimulates the appetite—so nibbling on a sweet snack to stave off hunger pangs may actually trigger overeating.

What about sugar's reputation as a good energy booster between meals? It's true that sugar is an inexpensive, easily digested energy source, but the same can be said for the far more nutritious complex carbohydrates (fruits, vegetables, whole-grain breads, etc.). Once consumed, these starches are converted into sugar (glucose) at a steady pace, keeping blood sugar—and energy—at an even level. Sugary snacks, on the other hand, tend to produce quick energy "peaks" which also fall quickly, leaving energy at a low ebb once more.

If your diet is high in sugar, begin cutting back:

- Use less sugar (granulated, brown, powdered and raw), syrups and honey.
- Choose fresh rather than canned fruit. If you buy canned fruit, select the water- or juice-packed type over fruit processed in heavy syrup.
- Limit your consumption of foods such as candy, soft drinks, ice cream, cakes and cookies.
- Read labels carefully; sugar has many names (see page 12).

AVOID TOO MUCH SODIUM

The average American consumes about 2 to 3 teaspoons of sodium a day. That is far too much, since the body needs only one-half (1/2) of a teaspoon daily to regulate the water balance. Too much sodium isn't good for anybody. It can be particularly bad for those with high blood pressure.

To reduce your daily sodium intake, start by learning where this element occurs in your diet. Surprisingly, you can consume an excess of sodium without even lifting a salt shaker. Sodium is found in products such as soy sauce, bouillon cubes and prepared mustard; it also hides in ketchup, salad dressings and breakfast cereals. Even foods that taste sweet are often high in sodium. Unlikely as it seems, one serving of chocolate cake made from a mix contains double the sodium of a 1-ounce serving of potato chips The explanation: In addition to plain salt, the cake mix contains baking powder and baking soda (both high in sodium) and disodium phosphates.

When you plan your menus, keep in mind that the Nutritional Research Council's "safe and adequate" daily sodium intake for an adult is 1,100 to 3,300 milligrams. Try to select foods that will keep your sodium intake to this level. For most of us, table salt is probably the major offender in excess sodium consumption, so using less salt is the most obvious way to cut down on sodium. If you're used to grabbing for the salt shaker, don't cut it out all at once; start with moderate changes.

Salting is a learned habit—and with effort, it can be unlearned. Here are four ways to shake the habit:

- Keep the salt shaker in the cupboard, not on the table.
- Reduce the salt in recipes by half.
- Season with lemon, wine vinegar, herbs and spices—experiment!
- Cut back on high-salt convenience foods.

DRINK ALCOHOLIC BEVERAGES IN MODERATION

Alcohol is low in nutritional value, rather high in calories and tends to interfere with the absorption of some nutrients (one reason why alcoholics often develop nutritional deficiencies). For these reasons, it's best to practice moderation in drinking. This is not to say you shouldn't drink at all; if you can afford the calories, an occasional glass of wine or a drink every now and then won't hurt you. In fact, a glass of white wine before dinner (80 to 100 calories) may sometimes enhance a weight-loss program by preventing the "diet deprivation syndrome." Just remember that wine is a food, and be sure to include it in your daily calorie total.

Some facts you should know:

- Use dry wines like chablis or vermouth for cooking. Unlike sweet wines, dry wines provide flavor with fewer calories.
- Beer loses its alcohol calories during cooking but leaves its carbohydrate calories, so select the "light" brands of beer for cooking.
- Distilled spirits like rum, Scotch and bourbon are great for cooking, leaving minimal calories and no carbohydrate calories.
- If the dish is not cooked the alcohol adds calories at about 100 per 3 ounces of wine or 1-1/2 ounces of distilled liquor.
- All hard liquors have comparable calorie counts. The higher a liquor's proof, the more alcohol and calories and the less real flavor it has.
- To metabolize 1 ounce of alcohol, the body requires 8 ounces of water. That's why the "morning after" is a thirsty day.

Nutrition Labeling

The most popular new word on package labels today is "lite." Supermarket shelves are lined with "lite" versions of countless products, from cheese to beverages to sausages to frozen dinners. We applaud the arrival of lighter, more healthful food which are a boon to nutrition-conscious consumers and those on special diets.

Just what do you get when you buy a "lite" or "light" food? What about "low-calorie" and "reduced-calorie" items? The Food and Drug Administration (FDA) standards specify that a product bearing the word "low-calorie" must have no more than 40 calories per serving or 0.4 calories per gram. A "reduced-calorie" food must have at least one-third fewer calories per serving than a "regular" version of the same food.

When it comes to "lite," the guidelines are less specific—though "lite" may be in, that doesn't always mean that calories are out. The FDA assumes that "lite" (or "light") means "light (low) in calories," *unless the label states otherwise*. Because the rules are not precise, a "lite" food may be low-calorie, reduced-calorie—or not even reduced in calories at all. Read "lite" labels carefully to see what you're getting, and don't be surprised to discover that some "lite" foods are just the same old products with different packaging and a new marketing strategy. For example, a "lite" corn chip has just one calorie less than a regular chip of the same brand, hardly worth the extra expense. Caution is also the rule in buying "natural" and "organic" foods. These two terms have never been defined by the Federal Trade Commission, and carry no guarantee of extra nutritional value.

Whatever food you buy, you can learn most about its nutritional value by reading the nutrition information on the package. U.S. government regulations require that this information be printed on the label for all fortified and enriched foods and for all foods claimed to have some specific nutritional characteristic ("low-sodium," for example). As shown in the sample milk label below, nutrition information is stated in two parts.

VITAMIN A & D SKIM MILK **GRADE A PASTEURIZED HOMOGENIZED** (Nutrition Information Per Serving)	
Serving size	1 cup
Servings per container	16
Calories	90
Protein	8 grams
Carbohydrate	12 grams
Fats	1 gram

Nutrition information per serving lists the number of calories and amounts of protein, carbohydrate and fats per serving. For skim milk, you can see that a 1 cup serving contains 90 calories and just 1 gram of fat.

PERCENTAGES OF US RECOMMENDED DAILY ALLOWANCES (US RDA)			
Protein	20	Niacin	*
Vitamin A	10	Calcium	30
Vitamin C	4	Iron	*
Thiamin	8	Vitamin D	25
Riboflavin	30	Vitamin B6	4
*Contains less than 2% of the US RDA of these nutrients.			

Percentages of U.S. Recommended Daily Allowances (RDA) are listed next. These are standards for daily nutrients set up by the Food and Nutrition Board of the U.S. Government. The figures for protein and seven vitamins and minerals must be listed in a specific order; figures for 12 other vitamins and minerals may or may not be listed, as the manufacturer chooses. The label above shows that skim milk is a good source of RDA for protein, riboflavin, calcium and vitamin D, but a poor source of iron, niacin and vitamin C.

If a product does not have a nutrition label, you can still learn something by reading the ingredient list. Ingredients are listed in order of quantity. If the first ingredient named is sugar, the product contains more sugar than it does any other ingredient.

SODIUM LABELING

If you're trying to cut down on sodium, learn to interpret those phrases you see on package labels— "low-sodium," "unsalted," and the like. "Low-salt" is one term you'll see frequently, often on such traditionally salty foods as potato chips, soups, margarine and soy sauce. Be aware that "low-salt" doesn't necessarily mean "low-sodium" since salt isn't the only cooking ingredient that contains sodium. Baking powder, baking soda, monosodium glutamate, sodium nitrate and sodium benzoate are all used in many foods, and all contain sodium. If a label states "no salt added," on the other hand, there's a better chance that the product is reduced in sodium. FDA rules require that "no salt added" cover *all* forms of sodium, not just salt.

How much sodium is in the processed foods we eat? The FDA requires that the sodium content of manufactured foods be included in the nutrition information listed as milligrams (mg) per serving. For specific claims about sodium content to appear on the label, the food must meet these standards:

● No Salt Added: No salt or any other form of sodium used in processing.
● Unsalted: Processed without salt; used to describe foods normally processed with salt (peanuts and canned vegetables, for example).
● Reduced Sodium: Processed to reduce the usual level of sodium by 75% or more.
● Low-Sodium: 140 mg sodium or less per serving.
● Very Low-Sodium: 35 mg sodium or less per serving.
● Sodium Free: Under 5 mg sodium per serving.

HIDDEN SUGARS

The low-sugar foods widely available today can be a boon to diabetics and weight-watchers. As always, however, caution is the rule when you buy. According to the FDA definition, "sugar" means only sucrose— ordinary table sugar. But since sucrose isn't the only form of sugar used in processing, foods labeled "low-sugar," "sugar-free" or "no sugar added" may well contain a fair amount of sweetener. Read product labels carefully and be on the lookout for sugar in *all* of its many forms.

SUGARS BY OTHER NAMES		
Corn syrup	Malt	Sorbitol
Dextrose	Maltose	Sucrose
Fructose	Mannitol	Syrup
Galactose	Mannose	Turbinade
Glucose	Molasses	Xylitol
Honey	Powdered sugar	Xylose
Lactose	Refined sugar	

SUGAR CONTENT OF BREAKFAST CEREALS	
Name of Cereal	% Sugar*
Sugar Smacks	56.0
Froot Loops	48.0
Raisin Bran	29.0
Bran Flakes	13.0
Wheaties	8.2
Rice Krispies	7.8
Grape-Nuts	7.0
Cornflakes	5.3
Corn Chex	4.0
Wheat Chex	3.5
Cheerios	3.0
Shredded Wheat	0.6
Puffed Rice	0.1
*All percentages based on 1979 USDA figures.	

If you're intent on reducing your sugar intake, you should obviously avoid sweets such as candy, cakes and cookies. Look for low-sugar (read the label!) versions of foods such as jams, preserves and condiments. Choose your breakfast cereal carefully, too. As the chart below illustrates, presweetened cereals aren't the only ones that may be fairly high in sugar. Select cereals that contain less than 13% sugar; many of the low-sugar types have been on the market for years. If you crave sweeter cereal, try adding sliced fresh fruit instead of sugar.

Finding Fats

Though fat is necessary in small amounts for good health (see page 8), too much fat can be bad for you. Nutritionists recommend limiting daily fat intake to 30% or less of the total calories consumed. Package labels usually list grams of fat per serving. To figure out the percentage of fat calories, use this simple formula:

$$\frac{(\text{grams of fat per serving}) \times (9 \text{ calories per gram of fat})}{\text{total calories per serving}}$$

For example, suppose you want to figure out the percent of fat calories in regular cottage cheese. The label tells you that a 1/2 cup serving contains 120 calories and 5 grams of fat. Applying the formula above, you find that regular cottage cheese gets (5) X (9) ÷ 120 = 37.5% of its calories from fat. Low-fat cottage cheese, on the other hand, has just 2 grams of fat and 100 calories in a 1/2 cup serving. For this product, only (2) X (9) ÷ 100 = 18% of the calories come from fat.

Limit your intake of all fats—be especially sparing in your consumption of saturated fats, as they may lead to a buildup of cholesterol in the body. Avoid fatty meats, butter, cream, palm and coconut oils and other foods high in saturated fat. Also look for foods labeled "no cholesterol," but keep in mind that "no cholesterol" does not mean "no fat." A number of no-cholesterol foods— such as peanut butter, vegetable shortenings and non-dairy coffee creamer—are nonetheless high in total fat or saturated fat. When you read labels, also be on the lookout for hydrogenated or partially hydrogenated fats. These, too, should be avoided. Hydrogenation is a process that changes liquid fats to solid ones—that is, it makes fats more saturated.

Cutting down on fat means choosing low-fat versions of favorite foods. Select luncheon meats labeled 96%, 97% or 98% fat-free (or choose those that have only 1 to 3 grams of fat per 2-ounce serving). Buy ice milk instead of ice cream. You'll find that strawberry ice milk tastes much more like berries than strawberry ice cream—and a 1-cup serving gets only 50 of its calories from fat, as

opposed to 180 fat calories in a 1-cup serving of ice cream. The chart at right shows fat calories in relation to total calories for certain favorite foods.

AMOUNT OF FAT CALORIES COMPARED TO TOTAL CALORIES			
Food	Serving Size	Calories	Fat Calories
Almonds	10	60	50
Avocado	1/2 medium	140	130
Bacon	2 slices	90	70
Bologna	1 oz.	80	60
Cheddar cheese	1 oz.	110	80
Part-skim mozzarella	1 oz.	79	54
Farmers cheese	1 oz.	45	5
Cream cheese	1 oz.	120	100
Chocolate bar	1.4 oz.	150	80
All-beef frankfurter	2 oz.	184	153
Ice cream	1 cup	260	180
Ice milk	1 cup	200	50
Whole milk	1 cup	160	80
Skim milk	1 cup	90	9
Salad dressings	1 tablespoon	100	100
Dairy sour cream	1 tablespoon	25	20
Plain low-fat yogurt	1 cup	150	70

Calcium Counts

Though we may outgrow our desire for milk, our bodies never outgrow the need for calcium. This mineral helps build strong bones and is important for proper blood clotting and nerve regulation. Inadequate calcium in the diet can lead to osteoporosis, a disease causing bone deterioration.

Milk, yogurt and other dairy products are our best sources of calcium. Unfortunately, many dieters trim calories by eliminating dairy products from their meals. A healthier alternative—one that keeps plenty of calcium in the diet—is to choose low-fat dairy products such as farmers cheese, skim milk and ice milk.

The RDA for calcium is 800 mg. Packaged foods carrying nutrition information on the label will always include RDA information for calcium; for example, the sample label on page 11 shows that one 8-ounce serving of skim milk supplies 30% of the RDA for calcium. The chart on page 14 gives milligrams of calcium per serving for a number of high-calcium foods, both packaged and fresh. Count up the calcium in your diet. If you're coming up short, boost your intake now. Here are a few ways to add calcium to your life:

• Drink cocoa instead of coffee or tea.

- Add instant nonfat dry milk to soups, sauces, stews and casseroles.
- For a great snack, eat plain yogurt and add fresh fruit; or enjoy low-fat cheeses and crackers.
- Make refreshing fruit milkshakes—get calcium and an energy boost, too.
- Create calcium-rich desserts such as puddings and custards with skim milk.
- Prepare canned soups with skim milk, not water.

CALCIUM CONTENT OF VARIOUS FOODS

Foods	Serving Size	Calcium (mg)
Dairy Products		
Milk, low-fat	1 cup	300
Milk, skim	1 cup	302
Ice cream or ice milk	1/2 cup	88
Cheese, Cheddar	1 oz.	204
Cheese, Swiss	1 oz.	272
Cheese, cottage, low-fat	1/2 cup	77
Yogurt, plain low-fat	1 cup	133
Vegetables & Fruits		
Bok choy, uncooked	1/2 cup	126
Collards, uncooked	1/2 cup	179
Kale, cooked	1/2 cup	103
Turnip greens, cooked	1/2 cup	126
Rhubarb, frozen, uncooked	1/2 cup	133
Legumes & Seafood		
Beans, dried, cooked	1 cup	90
Oysters, uncooked	7-9	113
Salmon, canned, with bones	3-1/2 oz.	372
Shrimp, canned	3 oz.	99
Tofu	4 oz.	145
Miscellaneous		
Molasses, blackstrap	1 tablespoon	137

of other basic nutrients. Concentrate on the first four groups as basics; select four servings a day from groups one and two, two to four servings from group three (dairy products); then add two servings from group four to balance the day's nutrition. If you can afford the extra calories, feel free to enjoy a daily serving from group five: fats, sweets or alcohol.

Eating the number of servings suggested from groups one through four will supply you with about 1,200 to 1,500 calories per day, depending on your intake from the dairy products group. Active adults, teens and children will require additional calories balanced from all the food groups.

DAILY FOOD GROUP GUIDE

Nutrients	Serving Size	Servings Per Day
Vegetables & Fruits		
Vitamins	1/2 cup juice, or	4 servings
A and C,	1 cup uncooked, or	
Minerals,	1/2 cup cooked	
Fiber		
Breads, Cereals, Legumes & Grain Products		
B vitamins,	1 slice bread,	4 servings
Fiber,	1/2 cup cereal,	
Iron	legumes or grain	
Dairy Products		
Calcium,	1 cup milk	2 servings (adults)
Riboflavin,	or yogurt, or	3 servings (teens)
Protein	1 oz. cheese	4 servings (children)
Meats, Poultry, Fish & Eggs		
Protein,	2 ounces	2 servings
Iron	1 egg	
Fats, Oils, Sweets & Alcohol		
Calories	1 tablespoon	*

*Choose only if you can afford the calories.

Menu Planning Using the Five Food Groups

One of the simplest ways to assure good health and nutrition is to plan meals around the five food groups: vegetables and fruits; breads, cereals, legumes and grain products; dairy products (low-fat cheese, low-fat or skim milk and yogurt); meats, poultry, fish and eggs; and fats, oils, sweets and alcohol.

Selecting a variety of foods from these groups will improve the nutrition on your plate and keep mealtime interesting. To make meal planning easy for you, we've set up a daily food group guide (at right). The guide takes into account the RDA for protein, calcium and a number

When you plan your menus, try setting up a whole week's worth of meals. Composing menus in "blocks" is a sure way to guarantee good nutrition for your family. By knowing what's planned for each day in the week, you'll more easily attain your health goals. And, be sure to keep meals interesting and attractive by including a variety of colors, flavors, textures and temperatures in each menu.

To start you off on creative meal planning we offer a few sample menus at right. All feature delicious dishes prepared quickly and nutritiously with the microwave oven. In today's hurry-up world, it's reassuring to know that healthy eating is a quick, easy choice. Enjoy!

Sample Menus

SUNDAY BRUNCH
Orange Wedges
Creamy Scrambled Eggs, page 18
Breakfast Home Fries, page 22
Cinnamon-Raisin Muffins, page 28

SPECIAL GUEST MENU
Skinny Shrimp Scampi, page 60
Quick Brown Rice, page 103
Broccoli with Herb Sauce, page 85
Strawberry Glacé Pie, page 126

UNDER 30 MINUTES
Meatza Pies, page 79
Teddy's Taters, page 94
Tomatoes & Zucchini, page 116
Easy Peach Cobbler, page 157

FAMILY DINNER
Savory Lamb Steaks, page 82
Zucchini Parmesan, page 151
Dilled New Potatoes, page 108
Crustless Blueberry Pie, page 128

PARTY APPETIZERS
Potato Skins, page 142
Spinach Balls, page 140
Crunchy Vegetable Rounds, page 141
"Fried" Zucchini or Mushrooms, page 139
Delicious Almond-Cheese Ball, page 144

Using the Recipes

Each of the recipes in this book has been carefully analyzed using a nutritional data base. The bar chart following each recipe represents, in grams, the percentage of carbohydrate, protein and fat calories per serving or item. In addition, the low-salt chapter includes sodium content in milligrams listed with each serving. Unless stated otherwise, each calorie count given is *per serving, or item,* as in the case of canapes, hors d'oeuvres and muffins.

As recommended by the U.S.D.A., nutrients should be consumed on a daily basis in these proportions: 58% carbohydrate (48% complex and 10% simple or refined sugars), 12% protein, and 30% fat (10% polyunsaturated, 10% monounsaturated, 10% saturated).

Please use the nutrient information as a guideline because discrepancies can occur due to variety, season, freshness and brand.

Corn Muffins

94 Calories/muffin ——— 1

A great muffin to serve as a snack or with a small bowl of chili.

1/2 cup yellow cornmeal	**1 tablespoon sugar**
1/2 cup all-purpose flour	**1/2 cup buttermilk**
1 teaspoon baking powder	**1 egg, lightly beaten**
1/2 teaspoon baking soda	**2 tablespoons vegetable oil**

Place a paper baking cup in cups of a microwave muffin ring or custard cups. In a medium bowl, combine cornmeal, flour, baking powder, baking soda and sugar. Mix in buttermilk, egg and oil. Fill cups half full. Microwave on 100% power (HIGH) as follows or until tops spring back when lightly touched.

1 muffin:	45 seconds	4 muffins:	2 minutes
2 muffins:	1 minute	5 muffins:	2 minutes 15 seconds
3 muffins:	1 minute 15 seconds	6 muffins:	2 minutes 30 seconds

Rotate muffin ring or custard cups halfway through cooking. Remove from muffin ring or custard cups to a wire rack; cool. Makes 9 (76 mg sodium) muffins. ——— 2
——— 3

4 ——— **Carbohydrate 11.8 g**
5 ——— **Protein 2.4 g**
6 ——— **Fat 4.2 g**

The following sample shows how to interpret each recipe:

1. Calories per serving or item (unless stated otherwise).
2. Number of servings or items (unless stated otherwise).
3. Sodium per serving in milligrams.
4. Carbohydrate per serving in grams.
5. Protein per serving in grams.
6. Fat per serving in grams.

Here are some helpful nutritional tips to get you started. You'll find more tips scattered through the next 9 chapters.

Most Americans consume an average of 15 grams dietary fiber a day. Nutritionists suggest we eat at least double this amount (30 grams daily).

The right way to increase fiber intake is to increase the amount (and the types) of high-fiber foods you eat. The wrong way is to take bran pills, dose yourself with bulk-forming laxatives, or rely solely on a sprinkle of bran atop low-fiber foods. To boost your daily fiber intake by 20 grams, include the following foods in the day's meals: 1/2 cup bran cereal, 2 slices whole wheat bread, 1 potato, 1 apple and 1 spear of broccoli.

Perfect as a snack or main-meal component for dieters, apples are filling food because of their high fiber and water content. They're not fattening, though; a medium apple provides only about 80 calories.

For substantial calorie savings, use plain yogurt instead of dairy sour cream in soups and sauces. Plain low-fat yogurt has only 8 calories per tablespoon; dairy sour cream measures in at 25 calories per tablespoon.

The calorie content of regular ground beef consists of about 30% fat so select the lean beef or, better yet, substitute ground turkey.

When you're hungry for something sweet, select the natural dessert, fruit—high in vitamins, low in fat.

Breakfast skippers tend to drag through the day, cultivating ravenous appetites that lead to nighttime overeating and inevitable weight gain.

Have mini-meals throughout the day rather than one or two big ones to keep blood sugar level balanced and increase metabolism to burn calories more efficiently.

It has been shown that middle-aged people tend to lose muscle mass at the rate of three to four percent every five years. This rate is accelerated in those people who are not physically active.

Walking is an excellent way to exercise. Regular walking improves health and reduces the incidence of heart disease.

Legumes are high in iron. To get the most from them, team them with foods rich in vitamin C, such as bell peppers, tomatoes or citrus fruits. By eating vitamin C and iron together, you'll absorb more of each nutrient.

Be sodium smart. Shake on the spices and leave the salt behind.

Entertain the healthy way by choosing low-fat entrees, such as fish, chicken or turkey.

Breakfast & Brunch

Beginning the day is so easy with your microwave. Simple dishes like Egg Burrito, Nutrition in a Bowl and Potato & Turkey Sausage Bake can be made in just minutes. And you needn't pass up traditional favorites—we've taken special care to provide low-fat versions of those high-fat classics. Try Creamy Scrambled Eggs and Breakfast Home Fries for an old-fashioned Sunday breakfast, and don't forget to pass the muffins—you'll find four kinds to choose from! Or create a winning brunch with everyone's favorite French Toast and a selection of homemade toppings. Micro-waved Blueberry Sauce, Cherry Sauce and Maple Syrup have all the flavor of the traditional syrup with far less fat and calories.

What if you just can't face food first thing in the morning? You'll do yourself a favor if you at least eat a piece of fruit or a simple food like Cinnamon-Raisin Muffins. For decades, researchers have reported that breakfast eaters show improved mental function and increased energy compared to those who skip the morning meal. Studies also reveal that eating breakfast helps you lose weight. By satisfying your body's nutritional needs early in the day, you'll avoid nighttime bingeing.

A good breakfast means a good start to the day—and your microwave makes great beginnings a snap!

Creamy Scrambled Eggs

A protein-packed way to start the day.

4 eggs, beaten
1 (3-oz.) package Neufchâtel cheese,
  cut in cubes
1/4 cup skim milk

1/2 green bell pepper, seeded, diced
1/4 teaspoon garlic powder
Dash black pepper

In a 1-1/2-quart microwave-safe casserole dish, combine eggs, cheese, milk, bell pepper, garlic powder and black pepper. Microwave on 70% power (MEDIUM-HIGH) 5 to 7 minutes, stirring every minute during cooking. When done, eggs should still look wet. Let stand 1 minute. Makes 4 servings.

Carbohydrate 2.5 g	
Protein 9.3 g	
Fat 11.4 g	

Egg & Sausage Strata

For low cost, high nutrition and versatility, eggs and cheese are hard to beat.

1 (16-oz.) package turkey breakfast sausage
4 eggs, beaten
1 teaspoon dry mustard
1-1/3 cups skim milk
5 slices bread, cut in cubes

2/3 cup shredded part-skim mozzarella
  cheese (2-2/3 oz.)
1/3 cup shredded sharp Cheddar cheese
  (1-1/3 oz.)

Coat a 1-1/2-quart microwave-safe casserole dish with cooking spray. In a medium microwave-safe bowl, microwave turkey sausage on 100% power (HIGH) 4 to 6 minutes, stirring several times during cooking. Drain; set aside. In a 4-cup glass measure, combine eggs, mustard and milk. Set aside. Spread bread cubes evenly over bottom of prepared dish. Spoon sausage over bread crumbs; sprinkle with mozzarella cheese. Pour milk mixture over top. Cover tightly. Refrigerate 4 to 12 hours. Uncover; microwave on 70% power (MEDIUM-HIGH) 12 to 16 minutes or until set. Sprinkle with Cheddar cheese. Makes 8 servings.

Carbohydrate 10.7 g	
Protein 16.3 g	
Fat 14.6 g	

How to Make an Egg Burrito

1/Beaten egg cooked with green onions and cherry tomato slices is spooned down center of flour tortilla.

2/Tortilla is rolled to enclose filling, topped with cheese and heated briefly in microwave.

Egg Burrito

243 Calories without salsa

Four food groups in one easy recipe.

1 egg, beaten
1/4 cup chopped green onions
2 cherry tomatoes, cut in quarters

1 (7-inch) flour tortilla
2 tablespoons shredded sharp Cheddar cheese
Salsa, if desired

In a 2-cup glass measure, combine egg, green onions and tomatoes. Microwave on 100% power (HIGH) 30 seconds. Stir; microwave on 100% power (HIGH) 30 seconds more. Spoon egg mixture in center of tortilla. Sprinkle with 1 tablespoon cheese. Roll up; place on a microwave-safe plate, seam-side down. Sprinkle with remaining 1 tablespoon cheese. Microwave on 100% power (HIGH) 30 seconds or until cheese is melted. Serve with salsa, if desired. Makes 1 serving.

Carbohydrate 23 g	
Protein 13.5 g	
Fat 12 g	

Tip

Eggs are an excellent source of protein, and they're low in calories and sodium.

Potato & Turkey Sausage Bake

182 Calories

A quick breakfast idea using low-fat turkey sausage.

2 medium (3-1/2-oz.) red
   thin-skinned potatoes,
   scrubbed, cut in wedges

1/2 (16-oz.) package turkey breakfast sausage
1/2 teaspoon dried leaf thyme

Arrange potato wedges around outside of a shallow 1-1/2-quart microwave-safe casserole dish. Crumble turkey sausage evenly in center of casserole dish. Sprinkle potatoes with thyme. Cover tightly. Microwave on 100% power (HIGH) 3 minutes. Stir; microwave on 100% power (HIGH) 3 minutes more or until potatoes are fork-tender. Makes 4 servings.

Carbohydrate 17.4 g	
Protein 9 g	
Fat 8 g	

Blueberry-Bran Muffins

125 Calories/muffin

Bran is considered synonymous with fiber.

1/4 cup vegetable oil
1 cup Bran Flakes
2/3 cup skim milk
1 egg
1 cup all-purpose flour
1/4 teaspoon salt

1 teaspoon baking powder
1/4 teaspoon baking soda
1/3 cup packed brown sugar
1 cup fresh or thawed frozen blueberries
1 teaspoon all-purpose flour

Line 6 cups of a microwave muffin ring or 6 custard cups with a paper baking cup. In a large bowl, combine oil, Bran Flakes, milk and egg. Let stand 5 minutes or until Bran Flakes are softened. Stir in 1 cup flour, salt, baking powder, baking soda and brown sugar. In a small bowl, toss blueberries with l teaspoon flour. Fold blueberries into batter. Fill muffin cups half-full with batter. If using custard cups, arrange in a circle in microwave oven. Microwave 100% power (HIGH) 1 minute. Rotate muffin ring or custard cups 1/2 turn. Microwave on 100% power (HIGH) 1 to 2 minutes more or until tops spring back when lightly touched. Remove from muffin ring or custard cups to a wire rack; cool. Repeat procedure with remaining batter. Makes 12 muffins.

Carbohydrate 17.6 g	
Protein 2.4 g	
Fat 5.4 g	

Applesauce-Spice Muffins

70 Calories/muffin

The cinnamon topping gives them beautiful brown tops.

3/4 cup baking mix
1 tablespoon sugar
1/4 teaspoon baking soda
1/4 teaspoon ground cinnamon
1/4 teaspoon ground nutmeg
1/8 teaspoon ground cloves

1/3 cup unsweetened applesauce
2 tablespoons skim milk
1 egg
2 teaspoons sugar
1 teaspoon ground cinnamon

Line each cup of a microwave muffin ring or custard cups with a paper baking cup. In a 4-cup glass measure, combine baking mix, 1 tablespoon sugar, baking soda, 1/4 teaspoon cinnamon, nutmeg and cloves. Stir in applesauce, milk and egg. Fill muffin cups half-full with batter. In a custard cup, combine 2 teaspoons sugar and 1 teaspoon cinnamon. Sprinkle evenly on top of each muffin. If using custard cups, arrange in a circle in microwave oven. Microwave on 100% power (HIGH) 1 minute. Rotate muffin ring or custard cups 1/2 turn. Microwave on 100% power (HIGH) 1 to 2 minutes more or until tops spring back when lightly touched. Remove from muffin ring or custard cups to a wire rack; cool. Makes 7 muffins.

Carbohydrate 10.9 g	
Protein 1.6 g	
Fat 2.2 g	

Tip

One egg yolk contains 270 milligrams of cholesterol. Most doctors recommend 300 milligrams of cholesterol a day.

Good Morning Omelet

138 Calories

Help yourself to fiber in the morning.

1 medium (5-1/2-oz.) red
  thin-skinned potato, scrubbed, pierced
4 eggs, beaten
1/2 cup chopped green onions
1/2 cup sliced fresh mushrooms

1/4 teaspoon dried leaf basil
1/8 teaspoon dried leaf oregano
Salt to taste
1 teaspoon margarine
1 small tomato, seeded, chopped

Place a paper towel on bottom of microwave oven. Microwave potato on 100% power (HIGH) 3 minutes. Cool and dice (do not peel). In a medium bowl, combine potato, eggs, green onions, mushrooms, basil, oregano and salt. Set aside. In a 9-inch microwave-safe pie plate, microwave margarine on 100% power (HIGH) 20 seconds or until melted. Swirl dish to coat. Pour egg mixture into pie plate. Adjust power level to 50% power (MEDIUM). Microwave 3 to 6 minutes or until edges look slightly set. Using a rubber spatula, gently lift edges of omelet, allowing uncooked egg to flow underneath. Sprinkle with tomato. Microwave on 50% power (MEDIUM) 3 to 5 minutes more or until set but still moist. Makes 4 servings.

Carbohydrate 10.9 g	
Protein 8.2 g	
Fat 7.5 g	

Breakfast Home Fries

83 Calories

You'll think these are right off the grill.

1/2 teaspoon margarine
1/4 cup chopped onion
1/2 teaspoon browning sauce
1/2 teaspoon garlic powder

1/4 teaspoon dried leaf thyme
1/2 teaspoon paprika
2 medium (5-1/2-oz.) baking
  potatoes, peeled, cut in 1/2-inch cubes

In a 1-1/2-quart microwave-safe casserole dish, combine margarine, onion, browning sauce, garlic powder, thyme and paprika. Microwave on 100% power (HIGH) 20 seconds or until margarine is melted. Coat potatoes in margarine mixture. Microwave on 100% power (HIGH) 8 to 9 minutes or until potatoes are fork-tender, stirring potatoes every 2 minutes during cooking. Makes 4 servings.

Carbohydrate 17.9 g	
Protein 2.3 g	
Fat 0.6 g	

Good Morning Omelet, Breakfast Home Fries and fresh fruit

Cinnamon & Orange Coffeecake

247 Calories

Orange juice adds to the sweetness of this coffeecake.

2 tablespoons chopped walnuts
1 tablespoon sugar
1/4 teaspoon ground cinnamon
1/3 cup margarine, softened
1/3 cup packed brown sugar
1 egg, lightly beaten
1-1/2 cups all-purpose flour
1 teaspoon baking powder

1/2 teaspoon baking soda
1/4 teaspoon salt
1/2 teaspoon ground cinnamon
2/3 cup orange juice
1/3 cup raisins
1/4 cup sifted powdered sugar
1 teaspoon orange juice

Coat a 1-1/2 quart microwave-safe ring pan with cooking spray. In a small bowl, combine walnuts, 1 tablespoon sugar and 1/4 teaspoon cinnamon. Sprinkle in bottom of prepared pan. In a medium bowl, cream margarine, brown sugar and egg. Stir in flour, baking powder, baking soda, salt, cinnamon and 2/3 cup orange juice. Fold in raisins. Pour batter into prepared pan. Place pan on an inverted microwave-safe pie plate in microwave oven. Microwave on 50% power (MEDIUM) 4 minutes. Rotate pan 1/2 turn. Microwave on 50% power (MEDIUM) 4 to 5 minutes more or until top springs back when lightly touched. Immediately invert on a wire rack. Let stand 10 minutes. Place on a serving plate. In a small bowl, combine powdered sugar and 1 teaspoon orange juice. Drizzle over coffeecake. Makes 8 servings.

Carbohydrate 37.8 g	
Protein 6.8 g	
Fat 9.7 g	

Nutrition in a Bowl

141 Calories

Package in individual self-sealing plastic bags for quick and easy serving.

1 cup instant nonfat dry milk powder
1/2 cup oat bran
2/3 cup quick-cooking rolled oats
1/4 cup raisins

1/4 cup chopped dried apricots
1 teaspoon salt
1 teaspoon ground cinnamon

In a large bowl, mix dry milk powder, oat bran, oats, raisins, apricots, salt and cinnamon. Package in individual plastic bags or a covered container. Makes enough cereal mix for 8 servings.

To make 1 serving, combine 1/3 cup cereal mix and 2/3 cup water in a deep microwave-safe cereal bowl. Microwave on 100% power (HIGH) 2 to 3 minutes, stirring every minute during cooking. Let stand 2 minutes.

Carbohydrate 29 g	
Protein 7.3 g	
Fat 0.7 g	

Breakfast Wedges

These high-fiber, fruity coffeecake wedges are great to take to work for breakfast or a snack.

1-1/2 cups quick-cooking rolled oats
3/4 cup all-purpose flour
1/2 cup packed brown sugar
1/2 teaspoon baking soda
1/4 teaspoon salt
1/4 teaspoon ground nutmeg
1 (8 oz.) can crushed pineapple

1/3 cup vegetable oil
1 egg
1 teaspoon vanilla
1 medium banana, mashed (1/2 cup)
1 teaspoon lemon juice
1/4 cup sifted powdered sugar

Coat a round 9-inch microwave-safe dish with cooking spray. In a medium bowl, combine oats, flour, brown sugar, baking soda, salt and nutmeg. Drain pineapple; reserve juice. Stir in 5 tablespoons pineapple (reserve remaining tablespoon for topping), oil, egg, vanilla, banana and lemon juice. Spread batter in prepared dish. Place dish on an inverted microwave-safe pie plate in microwave oven. Microwave on 50% power (MEDIUM) 4 minutes. Rotate dish 1/2 turn. Microwave on 50% power (MEDIUM) 3 to 4 minutes more or until a wooden pick inserted in center comes out clean. Cool on a wire rack. In a small bowl, combine powdered sugar, 1 teaspoon of reserved pineapple juice and reserved pineapple. Spread over coffeecake while still warm. Cool 10 minutes. Makes 16 wedges.

Carbohydrate 19.8 g		
Protein 2.4 g		
Fat 5.6 g		

Tip

Whole-grain products, such as rolled oats, oat bran and bran flakes, are high in B vitamins, which help control stress. (You'll find oat bran in the cereal section of your supermarket, alongside the rolled oats and other cooked cereals.)

Refrigerator Bran Muffins

96 Calories/muffin

A quick breakfast for the person on the run.

1/2 cup water
1/3 cup vegetable oil
1 cup whole bran cereal
1 large shredded wheat biscuit, crushed
1/2 cup packed brown sugar

1 egg, beaten
1 cup buttermilk
1-1/4 cups all-purpose flour
1 teaspoon baking soda
1/4 teaspoon salt

In a glass measure, microwave water on 100% power (HIGH) 1 minute or until boiling. In a large bowl, combine water, oil, bran cereal and wheat biscuit. Let stand 5 minutes or until cereals are softened. Stir in brown sugar, egg and buttermilk. Sift in flour, baking soda and salt. Stir just until dry ingredients are moistened. If desired, refrigerate batter tightly covered up to 1 month. To make muffins, line each cup of a microwave muffin ring or custard cups with a paper baking cup. Fill each cup with 2 tablespoons of batter. If using custard cups, arrange in a circle in microwave oven. Microwave on 100% power (HIGH) as follows or until tops spring back when lightly touched.

1 muffin:	45 seconds	5 muffins:	2 minutes 30 seconds
2 muffins:	1 minute 15 seconds	6 muffins:	3 minutes
3 muffins:	1 minute 30 seconds	7 muffins:	4 minutes
4 muffins:	2 minutes		

Rotate muffin ring or custard cups halfway through cooking. Remove from muffin ring or custard cups to a wire rack; cool. Makes 12 muffins.

Carbohydrate 13.9 g	
Protein 1.8 g	
Fat 4.4 g	

Berry Delicious Jam

16 Calories/tablespoon

A low-sugar spread packed with vitamin C.

1 pint fresh strawberries, hulled (2 cups)
3 tablespoons sugar

2 tablespoons dry pectin
1-1/2 teaspoons lemon juice

In a large microwave-safe bowl or an 8-cup glass measure, combine strawberries, sugar, pectin and lemon juice. Microwave on 100% power (HIGH) 11 to 13 minutes or until clear, stirring several times during cooking. Refrigerate tightly covered up to 1 month; freeze tightly covered up to 1 year. Makes 2 cups.

Carbohydrate 3.4 g	
Protein 0.1 g	
Fat 0.1 g	

How to Make French Toast

1/Bread is dipped in beaten egg mixture and allowed to stand until mixture is completely absorbed.

2/French Toast, shown topped with Berry Delicious Jam, cooks to a golden brown in 2 minutes.

French Toast

141 Calories without topping

An American favorite made without frying.

1 egg, beaten
2 teaspoons skim milk
1 slice whole-wheat bread

1/4 teaspoon ground cinnamon
Topping, if desired

In a shallow bowl, combine egg and milk. Dip bread slice in egg mixture; turn until well coated. Let bread soak 1 minute. Place bread on a microwave-safe plate. Microwave on 70% power (MEDIUM-HIGH) 1 minute. Turn bread over. Microwave on 70% power (MEDIUM-HIGH) 1 minute more or until center of bread is set. Sprinkle with cinnamon. Serve with topping, if desired. Makes 1 serving.

Carbohydrate 12.1 g	
Protein 9.1 g	
Fat 7.2 g	

Cinnamon-Raisin Muffins

115 Calories/muffin

Nature's way to start the morning, with fiber and flavor in every bite!

1 cup All Bran
3/4 cup buttermilk
1/2 cup orange juice
3 tablespoons vegetable oil
1 egg, beaten
1/4 cup sugar

1-1/4 cups all-purpose flour
2 teaspoons ground cinnamon
1 teaspoon baking soda
1/4 teaspoon salt
1/2 cup raisins

Line each cup of a microwave muffin ring or custard cups with a paper baking cup. In a large bowl, combine All Bran, buttermilk, orange juice and vegetable oil. Let stand 5 minutes or until cereal is softened. Stir in egg and sugar. Sift in flour, cinnamon, baking soda and salt. Mix thoroughly. Stir in raisins. Fill muffin cups with 2 tablespoons of batter. If using custard cups, arrange in a circle in microwave oven. Microwave on 100% power (HIGH) 1 minute. Rotate muffin ring or custard cups 1/2 turn. Microwave on 100% power (HIGH) 1 to 2 minutes more or until tops spring back when touched. Remove from muffin ring or custard cups to a wire rack; cool. Repeat procedure with remaining batter. Makes 14 muffins.

Carbohydrate 19.4 g	
Protein 2.4 g	
Fat 3.7 g	

Maple Syrup

4 Calories/tablespoon

Use on your favorite pancakes or French toast.

1 teaspoon cornstarch
5 teaspoons sugar
1/4 teaspoon salt

1 cup cold water
2 teaspoons imitation maple flavoring

In a 2-cup glass measure, combine cornstarch, sugar, salt and cold water. Microwave on 100% power (HIGH) 2 to 3 minutes or until syrup is clear and thickened, stirring every minute during cooking. Stir in maple flavoring. Cool; refrigerate tightly covered. Makes 1 cup.

Carbohydrate 1 g	
Protein 0 g	
Fat 0 g	

Tip

When microwaving muffins, always remove them when tops are still shiny. If tops look dry, muffins may turn out rubbery after standing for a few minutes.

Fruit Bagels

138 Calories

Chewy, satisfying bagels have fewer calories than butter-laden croissants.

1 (3-oz.) package Neufchâtel cheese
1 tablespoon grated orange peel
1 tablespoon thawed frozen
   orange juice concentrate

4 teaspoons chopped almonds
4 bagels, cut in half, toasted
2 cups fresh strawberries or other berries

In a small microwave-safe bowl, microwave cheese on 30% power (MEDIUM-LOW) 1 minute or until softened. Blend in orange peel, orange juice concentrate and almonds. Spread each bagel half with 1/8 of cheese mixture. Top with 1/4 cup berries. Makes 8 servings.

Carbohydrate 19.5 g	
Protein 4.6 g	
Fat 4.5 g	

Cinnamon-Spiced Applesauce

180 Calories

Use crisp, juicy, mildly tart apples, such as McIntosh or Gravenstein.

6 medium McIntosh or Gravenstein apples,
   peeled, cored, sliced (6 cups)

3/4 teaspoon ground cinnamon
1/4 cup sugar

In a 2-quart microwave-safe casserole dish, combine apples and cinnamon. Cover tightly. Microwave on 100% power (HIGH) 8 to 9 minutes or until apples are fork-tender, stirring several times during cooking. Mash apples to desired consistency. Stir in sugar. Makes 4 (1/2-cup) servings.

Carbohydrate 32.5 g	
Protein 1.5 g	
Fat 1.3 g	

Cherry Sauce

Fruit sauces can be full-flavored without being loaded with sugar.

1 (16-oz.) package frozen unsweetened pitted dark sweet cherries
Water

1/4 cup sugar
1-1/2 teaspoons cornstarch
1 teaspoon lemon juice

Using a fork, puncture 1 end of cherry bag. Set bag in a microwave-safe bowl. Microwave on 100% power (HIGH) 3-1/2 minutes. Empty cherries into a strainer set over a 4-cup glass measure. Drain 5 minutes. Set cherries aside. Add enough water to cherry juice in glass measure to make 1 cup liquid. In a custard cup, mix sugar and cornstarch. Stir into cherry juice mixture. Microwave on 100% power (HIGH) 2 to 3 minutes or until clear and thickened, stirring every minute during cooking. Stir in lemon juice and cherries. Cool; refrigerate tightly covered. Makes 2-1/2 cups.

Carbohydrate 11.6 g	
Protein 0.4 g	
Fat 0 g	

Blueberry Sauce

This makes a great topping for breakfast waffles, pancakes, French toast—or ice milk or puddings.

1 cup fresh or frozen unsweetened blueberries
1 tablespoon cornstarch

1-1/2 tablespoons sugar
1/2 cup unsweetened grape juice

If using frozen blueberries, microwave blueberries in a 2-cup glass measure on 100% power (HIGH) 1 minute. Set aside. In a 4-cup glass measure, combine cornstarch, sugar and grape juice. Stir in blueberries. Microwave on 100% power (HIGH) 2-1/2 to 3 minutes or until syrup is clear and thickened, stirring every minute during cooking. Makes 1-1/2 cups.

Carbohydrate 2.8 g	
Protein 0.1 g	
Fat 0 g	

Light Meals & Snacks

Light meals are low in fat, salt, calories—but high in nutrition and flavor. These mini-meals are great for waist-watchers. Try teaming any soup in this book with Priceless Pizza or Quickie Quesadillas for a nutritious lunch or dinner at 300 calories or less. Say goodbye to purchased frozen low-cal dinners—whip up quick microwave light meals instead.

Are you a nibbler? You have lots of company—snacking is one of America's favorite pastimes. It can be a healthy habit, too. According to some research, people who eat four to six small snacks a day maintain their weight more easily than those who eat two large, calorie-laden meals daily. The idea is to have low-calorie, highly-nutritious nibbles. Snacks are not unhealthy if included when planning your day's food intake. So say "yes" to snacks, but nibble nutritiously. Avoid chips, soda and candy; these offer lots of fat, sugar and salt, but few health benefits. What's more, fatty and sugary snacks provide energy only for the moment, soon leaving you hungry and tired again. Wise nibblers pick snacks with staying power. Complex carbohydrates and protein make a winning combination, supplying long-lasting energy. Try Tuna Tostadas or Chicken Pita Sandwiches and experience the energy bonus of smart snacking!

Priceless Pizza

Using a browning dish ensures a crisp, brown crust.

1/4 pound extra-lean ground beef
2 tablespoons diced onion
2 tablespoons diced green
  bell pepper
1/3 cup unsalted tomato sauce

2 (7-inch) flour tortillas
1/4 cup shredded part-skim
  mozzarella cheese (1 oz.)
3 pitted ripe olives, chopped

In a microwave-safe plastic colander, combine beef, onion and bell pepper. Set colander in a microwave-safe bowl. Microwave on 100% power (HIGH) 1-1/2 minutes. Stir with a fork. Microwave on 100% power (HIGH) 1-1/2 minutes or until meat is no longer pink. In a small bowl, combine beef mixture and tomato sauce. Set aside. Preheat a browning dish on 100% power (HIGH) 3 minutes. Coat dish with cooking spray. Place a tortilla in browning dish; spread with meat mixture. Microwave on 100% power (HIGH) 1 to 2 minutes. Sprinkle with cheese; garnish with olives. Repeat procedure with remaining ingredients. Makes 2 servings.

Carbohydrate 18.3 g	
Protein 14.8 g	
Fat 9.7 g	

Beef Jerky

For uniform slices, ask the butcher to slice the flank steak.

1 pound flank steak, trimmed of excess
  fat, cut in 1/8-inch thick slices

2 teaspoons seasoned salt
1/2 teaspoon black pepper

Place 6 steak slices on a microwave-safe rack set in a microwave-safe dish. In a custard cup, combine seasoned salt and pepper. Sprinkle both sides of steak strips with salt mixture. Cover with a paper towel. Microwave on 70% power (MEDIUM-HIGH) 10 minutes or until meat begins to look brown and dry. Finish drying on a paper towel. Repeat procedure 3 times with remaining meat and salt mixture. Refrigerate covered up to 1 month. Makes 24 pieces.

Carbohydrate 0.1 g	
Protein 13.5 g	
Fat 3.2 g	

How to Make Super Sloppy Joes

1/Ground beef and onion are combined in a microwave-safe colander, allowing the meat to drain as it cooks. Drain off cooking juices and transfer cooked meat to another bowl.

2/To serve, spoon the sauced-and-seasoned meat mixture over hamburger buns and top with cheese strips.

Super Sloppy Joes

288 Calories

A quick and easy favorite.

3/4 pound extra-lean ground beef
3/4 cup diced onion
1 (8-oz.) can unsalted tomato sauce
1 tablespoon sweet pickle relish
1 teaspoon brown sugar
1 tablespoon cider vinegar

1 teaspoon Worcestershire sauce
1 teaspoon prepared mustard
2 hamburger buns
2 (1-oz.) slices low-fat Cheddar cheese,
   cut in 4 strips each

In a microwave-safe plastic colander, combine beef and onion. Set colander in a microwave-safe bowl. Microwave on 100% power (HIGH) 4 to 5 minutes or until meat is no longer pink, stirring several times with a fork during cooking. In a 1-1/2-quart microwave-safe dish, combine beef mixture, tomato sauce, pickle relish, brown sugar, vinegar, Worcestershire sauce and mustard. Microwave on 100% power (HIGH) 2 to 3 minutes or until heated through. Spoon beef mixture evenly over 4 bun halves. Crisscross 2 cheese strips on each. Makes 4 servings.

Carbohydrate 20.8 g	
Protein 22.6 g	
Fat 13.0 g	

Individual Italian Heroes

318 Calories

Great to fix when friends stop in. Serve with fresh fruit for a complete meal.

1/2 pound extra-lean ground beef
1 cup purchased meatless spaghetti sauce

4 frankfurter buns, split
4 (1-oz.) slices American cheese, cut in halves

Place beef in a microwave-safe plastic colander. Set colander in a microwave-safe bowl. Microwave on 100% power (HIGH) 1-1/2 minutes. Stir with a fork. Microwave on 100% power 1-1/2 minutes more or until meat is no longer pink. In a medium bowl, combine beef and spaghetti sauce. Set aside. Remove centers of buns to hollow halves slightly. Place buns, hollowed-side up, on a large microwave-safe plate. Fill with meat mixture. Top each filled bun half with 1/2 slice of cheese. Adjust power level to 50% power (MEDIUM). Microwave 2 to 3 minutes or until heated through. Makes 4 servings.

Carbohydrate 26.2 g	
Protein 19 g	
Fat 14.7 g	

Chicken Nuggets

269 Calories

Bite-sized appetizers with an Italian accent.

1 pound boned skinned chicken breasts,
  cut in 1-inch chunks
15 round butter crackers, finely crushed
1/4 cup grated Parmesan cheese
  (3/4 oz.)

1/2 teaspoon garlic powder
1 teaspoon paprika
1 teaspoon Italian seasoning
Lemon wedges

Line a microwave-safe plate with a paper towel. Rinse chicken in cold water; do not pat dry. Set aside. In a plastic bag, combine crackers, Parmesan cheese, garlic powder, paprika and Italian seasoning. Shake bag to mix. Add chicken chunks, several at a time. Shake to coat well. Arrange chicken on prepared plate. Microwave on 100% power (HIGH) 3 minutes. Rearrange, moving outside pieces to center of dish. Microwave on 100% power (HIGH) 3 to 4 minutes more. Serve with lemon wedges. Makes 4 servings.

Carbohydrate 18.0 g	
Protein 39.9 g	
Fat 8.6 g	

Chicken Pita Sandwiches

236 Calories

A complete nutritious meal in a pocket.

l ounce Neufchâtel cheese
1/2 cup shredded carrot
1/4 cup chopped celery
1/4 cup chopped green onions
1-1/2 cups chopped cooked chicken

1/4 teaspoon garlic powder
2 pita bread rounds, halved
1 cup torn spinach leaves
1/3 cup shredded Cheddar cheese
(1-1/3-oz.)

In a 1-quart microwave-safe dish, combine Neufchâtel cheese, carrot, celery and green onions. Microwave on 50% power (MEDIUM) 1-1/2 minutes or until cheese is softened. Stir in chicken and garlic powder. Line each pita half with 1/4 of spinach leaves; spoon 1/4 of filling into each pita half. Place sandwiches on a microwave-safe plate. Microwave on 50% power (MEDIUM) 1-1/2 minutes. Open each sandwich slightly; sprinkle with cheddar cheese. Makes 4 servings.

Carbohydrate 21.5 g	
Protein 21.1 g	
Fat 7.3 g	

Pineapple-Frankfurter Kabobs

143 Calories/kabob

These turkey frankfurters are basted with a sweet and sour glaze.

8 turkey frankfurters, cut in 1-inch chunks
to make 40 pieces
1 (15-1/4-oz.) can chunk pineapple
packed in unsweetened
pineapple juice

4 celery stalks, cut diagonally
in 1-inch slices to make 30 pieces
2 teaspoons cornstarch
1 tablespoon white wine vinegar

Drain pineapple, reserving 1/2 cup juice. Thread frankfurters on 10 wooden skewers alternately with pineapple and celery, using 4 frankfurter pieces, 5 pineapple chunks and 3 celery slices per skewer. Arrange crosswise on a microwave-safe rack set in an 11'' x 7'' microwave-safe dish. Set aside. In a 2-cup glass measure, combine reserved pineapple juice, cornstarch and vinegar. Microwave on 70% power (MEDIUM-HIGH) 1 minute. Stir; microwave on 70% power (MEDIUM-HIGH) 1 minute more or until clear and slightly thickened. Brush kabobs with 1/2 of sauce. Microwave on 70% power (MEDIUM-HIGH) 1 minute. Turn over; brush with remaining sauce. Microwave on 70% power (MEDIUM-HIGH) 1 to 2 minutes more. Makes 10 kabobs.

Carbohydrate 19 g	
Protein 3.9 g	
Fat 5.9 g	

Fiesta Taco Salad

250 Calories

High in potassium—great for the heart!

1 pound ground turkey
1 medium onion, diced
1/3 cup low-sodium lite ketchup
2 teaspoons chili powder
1 teaspoon ground cumin

1/4 teaspoon black pepper
6 cups shredded lettuce
2 large tomatoes, chopped
Red onion slices
Cilantro leaves

In a microwave-safe plastic colander, combine turkey and onion. Set colander in a microwave-safe bowl. Microwave on 100% power (HIGH) 5 to 7 minutes or until meat is no longer pink, stirring several times with a fork during cooking. In a medium bowl, combine turkey mixture, ketchup, chili powder, cumin and pepper. Microwave on 100% power (HIGH) 1 to 2 minutes or until hot. Arrange 1-1/2 cups of lettuce on each of 4 plates. Top each plate of lettuce with 1/4 of turkey mixture, tomatoes, red onion and cilantro. Makes 4 servings.

Carbohydrate 10.9 g	
Protein 40 g	
Fat 4.6 g	

Turkey Divinewiches

205 Calories

Fix this mini-meal in minutes. It's a great way to serve broccoli.

1 (10-oz.) package frozen broccoli spears
2 cups chopped cooked turkey
1 (10-3/4-oz.) can condensed Cheddar
   cheese soup

1 tablespoon minced onion
1/4 teaspoon black pepper
4 English muffins, split, toasted
8 cherry tomatoes, cut in halves

Remove broccoli from package. Place in a 1-quart microwave-safe dish. Cover tightly. Microwave on 100% power (HIGH) 6 minutes. Drain; set aside. In a 4-cup glass measure, combine turkey, soup, onion and pepper. Arrange muffins in a circle on a microwave-safe platter. Spoon 1/8 of broccoli over each muffin; top with 1/8 of turkey mixture. Microwave on 100% power (HIGH) 3 minutes or until bubbly. Garnish each muffin with 2 tomato halves. Makes 8 servings.

Carbohydrate 24.4 g	
Protein 15.8 g	
Fat 4.9 g	

Fiesta Taco Salad

Tuna Tostadas

309 Calories

Pinto beans are an excellent source of fiber.

1 (6-1/2-oz.) can white tuna,
   packed in water, drained
1/2 cup dairy sour cream
1/4 teaspoon chili powder
1/4 teaspoon onion powder
1 green onion, chopped
1 cup canned pinto beans,
   rinsed, drained, mashed

4 (7-inch) flour tortillas
1/2 cup shredded part-skim mozzarella
   cheese (2 oz.)
1 cup shredded lettuce
1 medium tomato, chopped

Line a microwave-safe plate with a paper towel. In a medium bowl, thoroughly mix tuna, sour cream, chili powder and onion powder. Stir in green onion. Spread 1/4-cup beans on each tortilla; top each with 1/4 of tuna mixture. Sprinkle each tostada with 2 tablespoons cheese. Place a tostada on prepared plate. Microwave on 50% power (MEDIUM) 2 minutes or until heated through. Repeat procedure with remaining tostadas. In a small bowl, toss lettuce and tomatoes. Sprinkle over tostadas. Makes 4 servings.

Carbohydrate 32.6 g	
Protein 23.7 g	
Fat 9.7 g	

Tasty Tuna Muffins

162 Calories

A brunch or lunch dish that's packed with protein.

1/2 cup diced green bell pepper
1/2 cup diced green onions
4 eggs, beaten
1 (6-1/2-oz.) can white tuna
   packed in water, drained

2 tablespoons skim milk
1/2 teaspoon garlic salt
4 English muffins, split, toasted
Spinach leaves
4 large pitted black olives, sliced

In a medium microwave-safe bowl, combine bell pepper and onions. Cover tightly. Microwave on 100% power (HIGH) 1 minute. Stir in eggs, tuna, milk and garlic salt. Adjust power level to 50% power (MEDIUM). Microwave 7 to 8 minutes or until thick and creamy, stirring every 2 minutes during cooking. Arrange spinach leaves on each muffin half. Spoon tuna mixture over spinach. Garnish with olive slices. Makes 8 servings.

Carbohydrate 18.9 g	
Protein 12.6 g	
Fat 4.5 g	

Cranberry-Nut Bread

117 Calories/slice

A great gift to give friends and neighbors at Christmas.

1/4 cup vegetable oil
1/2 cup sugar
1 egg
1/4 cup water
1 cup whole berry cranberry sauce
1 tablespoon grated orange peel

1 teaspoon vanilla extract
1-1/2 cups all-purpose flour
1 teaspoon baking powder
1 teaspoon ground cinnamon
1/3 cup chopped walnuts

Coat bottom and sides of a 9'' x 5'' microwave-safe loaf pan with cooking spray. In a large bowl, combine oil, sugar, egg and water. Stir in cranberry sauce, orange peel and vanilla. Mix in flour, baking powder and cinnamon. Stir in walnuts. Spread batter evenly in prepared pan. Shield corners with foil. Microwave on 50% power (MEDIUM) 9 to 10 minutes. Remove foil. Rotate pan 1/4 turn. Microwave on 100% power (HIGH) 1 to 2 minutes or until top is still slightly shiny and springs back when lightly touched. Cool 5 minutes. Remove from pan to a wire rack. Makes 16 (about 1/2-inch) slices.

Carbohydrate 15.4 g	
Protein 1.5 g	
Fat 5.4 g	

Cheesy Snacks

42 Calories/piece

Prepare and refrigerate up to 4 hours ahead, ready to heat, for a quick snack or party appetizer.

1 (3-oz.) package Neufchâtel cheese
1/4 cup chopped green onions
1/4 teaspoon celery seeds

1/4 teaspoon garlic powder
20 Melba toast rounds
Paprika

In a small microwave-safe bowl, microwave cheese on 30% power (MEDIUM-LOW) 1 minute or until softened. Blend in green onions, celery seeds and garlic powder. Spread 1 teaspoon of mixture on each toast round. Place 10 cheese rounds in a circle on a microwave-safe plate. Adjust power level to 50% power (MEDIUM). Microwave 1 minute or until warm. Sprinkle with paprika. Repeat procedure with remaining ingredients. Makes 20 pieces.

Carbohydrate 5.6 g	
Protein 1.3 g	
Fat 1.6 g	

Tip

Sandwiches can be power packed mini-snacks providing high protein, carbohydrates and little fat.

Fiesta Popcorn Snack

45 Calories

A high-fiber snack low in calories.

2 tablespoons margarine
1 tablespoon Worcestershire sauce
2-1/2 cups popped popcorn
3/4 cup bite-size shredded wheat

1 cup o-shaped toasted-oat cereal
1/2 teaspoon chili powder
1/2 teaspoon garlic powder
1/4 teaspoon ground cumin

In a 1-cup glass measure, microwave margarine and Worcestershire sauce on 100% power (HIGH) 55 to 60 seconds. In a large microwave-safe bowl, combine popcorn, shredded wheat and toasted oat cereal. Pour margarine mixture over all. Sprinkle with chili powder, garlic powder and cumin; toss well. Microwave on 100% power (HIGH) 4 to 5 minutes or until hot and crisp, stirring occasionally during cooking. Spread on a baking sheet until cool. Makes 8 (1/2-cup) servings.

Carbohydrate 6.2 g	
Protein 1 g	
Fat 1.9 g	

Quickie Quesadillas

175 Calories

A quick, colorful and well balanced snack, full of calcium and vitamin C.

3/4 cup shredded part-skim mozzarella
  cheese (3 oz.)
3/4 cup shredded Longhorn cheese (3 oz.)

6 (6-inch) corn tortillas
1 (4-oz.) can diced green chilies, drained
1 medium tomato, chopped

In a medium bowl, combine cheeses. Place a tortilla on a microwave-safe plate. Sprinkle with 1/4 cup of cheeses. Top with 1/6 of chilies and tomato. Microwave on 50% power (MEDIUM) 1 minute or until cheese is melted. Fold in 1/2. Repeat procedure with remaining ingredients. Makes 6 servings.

Carbohydrate 17.9 g	
Protein 9.5 g	
Fat 7.8 g	

Cheese Crisp

Using farmers cheese lowers fat calories.

1/4 cup shredded farmers cheese (1 oz.)
1/4 cup shredded Cheddar cheese (1 oz.)

1 (12-inch) flour tortilla
Salsa, if desired

In a medium bowl, combine cheeses. Place tortilla on a microwave-safe plate. Microwave on 100% power (HIGH) 1 minute. Rotate plate 1/2 turn. Microwave on 100% power (HIGH) 1 minute more or until crisp. Top with cheeses. Adjust power level to 70% power (MEDIUM-HIGH). Microwave 45 seconds to 1 minute or until cheese is melted. Cut in 4 wedges. Serve with salsa, if desired. Makes 4 servings.

Carbohydrate 3.6 g	
Protein 3.9 g	
Fat 4.9 g	

Chocolate Pudding

A rich, creamy dessert that's low in calories.

2 cups skim milk
1/4 cup sugar
2 tablespoons sifted unsweetened cocoa powder
2 tablespoons cornstarch

1/2 teaspoon butter flavoring
1 egg
1 teaspoon vanilla extract

In a 4-cup glass measure, microwave 1-1/2 cups milk on 100% power (HIGH) 2 to 3 minutes or until small bubbles appear around edges. In a small bowl, combine sugar, cocoa, cornstarch and remaining 1/2 cup milk. Stir until cornstarch dissolves. Stir mixture into hot milk. Stir in butter flavoring. Microwave on 100% power (HIGH) 2 minutes; stir with a whisk. In a medium bowl, beat egg; gradually add hot milk mixture, stirring constantly. Pour back into 4-cup measure. Microwave on 100% power (HIGH) 4 to 5 minutes or until thickened, stirring after every minute during cooking. Stir in vanilla; pour into 4 small dessert dishes. Cover with wax paper. Refrigerate until cold. Makes 4 servings.

Carbohydrate 25 g	
Protein 6.4 g	
Fat 2.5 g	

Lentil-Tomato Dish

76 Calories

Lentils are high in natural water-soluble fiber, adding bulk to the diet and helping keep the digestive tract healthy.

4 cups water
3/4 cup dried lentils
1 cup chopped onion
3 carrots, sliced
2 celery stalks, sliced
3/4 teaspoon salt
1/2 teaspoon black pepper

1-1/2 teaspoons lemon juice
1/4 cup chopped fresh parsley
1/4 teaspoon garlic powder
1/4 teaspoon dried leaf thyme
1 (6-oz.) can tomato paste

In a 4-quart microwave-safe dish, combine water, lentils, onion, carrots, celery, parsley, salt, pepper, lemon juice, garlic powder and thyme. Cover tightly. Microwave on 70% power (MEDIUM-HIGH) 40 minutes, stirring several times during cooking. Stir in tomato paste. Recover; microwave on 70% power (MEDIUM-HIGH) 5 to 10 minutes more or until mixture is as thick as desired, stirring several times during cooking. Makes 8 (3/4 cup) servings.

Carbohydrate 15.6 g	
Protein 4.2 g	
Fat 0.2 g	

Ham & Cheese Sandwiches

214 Calories

Dijon-style mustard gives this sandwich special flavor.

6 medium slices rye bread
Dijon-style mustard
6 (1-oz.) slices turkey ham

6 (2/3-oz.) slices Swiss-style
    low-fat processed cheese product
Poppy seeds

Place bread slices on a microwave-safe plate. Spread each slice with mustard. Top each bread slice with a turkey ham slice and a cheese slice. Sprinkle with poppy seeds. Microwave on 50% power (MEDIUM) 2 minutes or until cheese is melted. Makes 6 servings.

Carbohydrate 12 g	
Protein 19.9 g	
Fat 9.7 g	

Poultry

Poultry is one of the best protein sources. It is nutritious, economical and low in calories and cholesterol. For the most protein and the least fat and calories, choose young broiler-fryers instead of roasting chickens: the younger the bird, the leaner the meat. Among chicken pieces, the breast is your best choice. It offers lean, low-calorie meat with little fat and waste.

Turkey is tops for nutrition, too—and it's no longer just for Thanksgiving. Most turkeys are marketed young, so the ratio of calories to protein to fat is perfect for those trying to control fat intake. If you prefer not to buy a whole bird, you still have plenty of choices—most markets offer turkey parts, flavorful turkey sausage and ground turkey year round. Sold fresh or frozen, versatile ground turkey is a real bargain; it's lower in fat than regular ground beef and can substitute for ground beef in many recipes.

Microwaved poultry dishes offer a cook limitless variety with moist, tender, tasty results every time. Try Chicken Cordon Bleu or Tarragon Chicken for a company dinner; sample tasty Turkey Chili and elegant Turkey Scaloppine. Once you've tried the recipes in this chapter, invent your own microwaved poultry specialties. Low-calorie, nutritious meals never tasted better!

Tip: As poultry is low in fat and cooks so quickly in the microwave, it does not brown well. For good eye appeal, use a browning sauce or a seasoned coating mix.

Chicken Cordon Bleu

This recipe can be prepared early in the morning, then microwaved in under 15 minutes at dinner time.

4 (4-oz.) boneless chicken breast halves,
   skinned, pounded 1/4-inch thick
1/4 pound turkey ham, cut in 4 thin slices
2 (2/3-oz.) slices Swiss-style low-fat
   processed cheese product, cut in half
1/4 cup seasoned coating mix

1 teaspoon cornstarch
1/4 cup skim milk
2 tablespoons minced onion
6 fresh mushrooms, sliced
3 slices Swiss-style low-fat processed
   cheese product, diced (2-oz.)

Place 1 turkey ham slice half on each chicken breast. Top with a cheese slice half. Roll up chicken, tucking in sides. Secure with a wooden pick. Spread coating mix on a plate. Roll chicken in coating mix. Arrange in a 9-inch microwave-safe pie plate. Microwave on 100% power (HIGH) 5 minutes. Remove wooden picks. Turn chicken rolls over. Microwave on 100% power (HIGH) 3 minutes. Drain cooking juices into a 4-cup glass measure. In a small bowl, dissolve cornstarch in milk, making a paste. Stir into cooking juices. Stir in onion and mushrooms. Microwave on 100% power (HIGH) 2 to 3 minutes or until thick, stirring every minute during cooking. Stir in cheese until melted. Spoon over chicken. Adjust power level to 70% power (MEDIUM-HIGH). Microwave 1 to 2 minutes. Makes 4 servings.

Carbohydrate 9.1 g	
Protein 39.8 g	
Fat 7.5 g	

Turkey Chili

Ground turkey, with less fat and more protein, is a good substitute for ground beef. It's often found in the frozen meat section.

1 pound ground turkey
1 cup chopped onion
1/2 cup chopped green bell pepper
2 tablespoons chopped pimento

1 (16-oz.) can tomatoes
1 teaspoon chili powder
1/2 teaspoon black pepper
Dash red (cayenne) pepper

In a microwave-safe plastic colander, combine turkey, onion and bell pepper. Set colander in a microwave-safe bowl. Microwave on 100% power (HIGH) 5 to 6 minutes or until meat is no longer pink, stirring several times with a fork during cooking. In a medium microwave-safe bowl, combine turkey mixture, pimento, tomatoes with juice, chili powder, black pepper and red pepper. Cover tightly. Adjust power level to 50% power (MEDIUM). Microwave 13 minutes. Let stand 5 minutes. Makes 4 servings.

Carbohydrate 6.9 g	
Protein 18.6 g	
Fat 9.0 g	

How to Make Chicken Cordon Bleu

1/Chicken breasts are pounded to 1/4-inch thickness, topped with cheese and turkey ham, then rolled and secured with wooden picks.

2/Mushrooms, cheese, onion, and juices accumulated from cooking chicken are transformed into a seemingly-rich sauce which is spooned over poultry before serving.

Barbecued Chicken

244 Calories

Paprika adds to the color and flavor of this dish.

1 cup low-sodium lite ketchup	2 tablespoons packed brown sugar
1/4 cup cider vinegar	2 teaspoons paprika
1 tablespoon Worcestershire sauce	8 (3-1/2-oz.) boned chicken breasts,
1/4 cup chopped onion	skinned

In a 4-cup glass measure, combine ketchup, vinegar, Worcestershire sauce, onion, brown sugar and paprika. Microwave on 100% power (HIGH) 5 minutes, stirring twice during cooking. Set aside. Arrange chicken in a 13'' x 9'' microwave-safe dish with thickest parts to outside of dish. Cover tightly. Microwave on 100% power (HIGH) 10 minutes. Drain; rearrange, moving outside pieces to center of dish. Pour sauce over chicken. Recover; microwave on 100% power (HIGH) 10 to 12 minutes or until meat is cooked through (cut to test). Let stand 5 minutes. Makes 8 servings.

Carbohydrate 5.1 g	
Protein 38 g	
Fat 7.3 g	

Chicken Enchiladas

Traditional Mexican flavor in today's healthful style.

1 cup chopped onion
1 garlic clove, minced
1 (16-oz.) can tomatoes
1 tablespoon cornstarch
1 (4-oz.) can diced green chilies
1 (8-oz.) can tomato sauce
1/2 teaspoon ground cumin

2 cups diced cooked chicken
1/3 cup plain low-fat yogurt
1/4 cup chopped fresh parsley
8 (6-inch) corn tortillas
1/3 cup shredded sharp Cheddar cheese
  (1-1/3 oz.)

Place onion and garlic in a microwave-safe bowl. Cover tightly. Microwave on 100% power (HIGH) 1-1/2 minutes. Drain tomatoes, reserving juice. Stir cornstarch into tomato juice until dissolved; stir into onion mixture. Cut up tomatoes. Stir cut-up tomatoes, chilies, tomato sauce and cumin into onion mixture. Microwave on 100% power (HIGH) 4 to 5 minutes or until sauce bubbles and is slightly thickened, stirring every minute during cooking. Set aside. In a medium bowl, combine chicken, yogurt and parsley. Wrap tortillas in paper towels. Microwave on 100% power (HIGH) 1 minute to soften. Spread about 1/4 cup chicken mixture across lower 1/3 of each tortilla; roll up. Place rolled tortillas, seam-side down, in an 11'' x 7'' microwave-safe dish. Pour tomato-chili sauce over tortillas. Microwave on 100% power (HIGH) 4 to 6 minutes or until heated through. Sprinkle with cheese. Microwave on 100% power (HIGH) 1 minute or until cheese is melted. Makes 4 servings.

Carbohydrate 22.4 g	
Protein 17.8 g	
Fat 6.5 g	

Tip

Trying to stay away from saturated fat? Read labels on margarine packages. Choose margarine that lists as its primary ingredient liquid safflower, sunflower, corn or soybean oil; avoid products with partially hydrogenated oils. Hydrogenation is a process that converts liquid fats to solid ones—that is, it makes fats more saturated.

Tarragon Chicken

339 Calories

The microwave method of cooking produces extremely moist poultry.

1 (3 to 3-1/2 lb.) whole broiler-fryer
Garlic salt
Black pepper
1 celery stalk, cut in 2-inch pieces

1 small onion, cut in wedges
2 tablespoons margarine
2 tablespoons browning sauce
1 teaspoon dried leaf tarragon

Sprinkle chicken body cavity with garlic salt and pepper to taste. Stuff with celery and onion. Truss chicken, using nonmetal skewers. Place, breast down, on a microwave-safe rack set in a 11'' x 7'' microwave-safe dish. In a custard cup, microwave margarine on 100% power (HIGH) 45 seconds or until melted. Stir in browning sauce. Brush 1/2 of mixture over chicken. Sprinkle with tarragon. Cover with wax paper. Microwave on 100% power (HIGH) 12 minutes. Turn chicken over. Brush with remaining margarine mixture. Microwave on 100% power (HIGH) 6 to 8 minutes more or until juices run clear when bird is cut between breast and thigh. Makes 4 servings.

Carbohydrate 2.6 g	
Protein 49.0 g	
Fat 13.9 g	

Chinese Chicken Strips

384 Calories

Turn your microwave into a wok with this quick "stir-fry."

1 pound boned chicken breasts,
   skinned, cut in thin strips
3 tablespoons lite soy sauce
1/3 cup dry white wine
1/2 teaspoon ground ginger
1 tablespoon water
1-1/2 tablespoons cornstarch

1 medium onion, sliced
6 ounces fresh mushrooms, sliced (2 cups)
3-1/2 ounces fresh snow peas, ends and
   strings removed
1 tomato, cut in quarters
2 cups hot, cooked rice

Place chicken in a 2- to 3-quart microwave-safe dish. In a small bowl, combine soy sauce, wine and ginger. Pour over chicken; mix gently. Cover tightly. Refrigerate 1 to 2 hours. Drain soy sauce mixture from chicken into a small bowl. Add water to soy sauce mixture. Stir in cornstarch until completely dissolved. Add onion and mushrooms to chicken. Pour soy sauce mixture over chicken and vegetables; mix gently. Cover tightly. Microwave on 100% power (HIGH) 5 minutes. Stir; recover. Microwave on 100% power (HIGH) 4 to 5 minutes more or until sauce is thickened and chicken is no longer pink in centers (cut to test). Stir in snow peas and tomato. Recover; microwave on 100% power (HIGH) 2 minutes. Serve over rice. Makes 4 servings.

Carbohydrate 39.0 g	
Protein 42.5 g	
Fat 6.4 g	

Chicken Cacciatore

This is a traditional Italian favorite. For a complete meal, serve with a lettuce, cucumber and radish salad.

3 (8-oz.) whole chicken breasts,
  split, skinned
4 ounces fresh mushrooms, sliced (1-1/2 cups)
1/2 cup chopped onion
1/3 cup grated carrot
1 (15-oz.) can unsalted tomato sauce
1 teaspoon dried leaf oregano, or
  2 teaspoons chopped fresh oregano

1/4 teaspoon garlic powder
1/2 teaspoon crushed fennel seeds
1/4 teaspoon black pepper
Hot spaghetti squash, page 97
Fluted mushroom, if desired
Sprig fresh oregano, if desired

Arrange chicken in a 11'' x 7'' microwave-safe dish with thickest parts to outside of dish. Top with mushrooms. Set aside. In a 4-cup glass measure, combine onion and carrot. Cover tightly. Microwave on 70% power (MEDIUM-HIGH) 2 minutes. Stir in tomato sauce, oregano, garlic powder, fennel seeds and pepper. Pour over chicken. Cover tightly. Adjust power level to 70% power (MEDIUM-HIGH)). Microwave 8 minutes. Rearrange chicken pieces moving outside pieces to center of dish. Recover; microwave on 70% power (MEDIUM-HIGH) 8 to 10 minutes more or until chicken is no longer pink in thickest part (cut to test). Serve over spaghetti squash. Garnish with mushroom and sprig fresh oregano, if desired. Makes 6 servings.

Carbohydrate 53.5 g	
Protein 37.5 g	
Fat 6.8 g	

Turkey Scaloppine

As delicious as veal—and only half the price.

1 pound turkey breast slices
1 (15-oz.) can unsalted tomato sauce
2 tablespoons dry white wine
2 tablespoons Worcestershire sauce

1/2 teaspoon fennel seeds, crushed
1/2 teaspoon dried leaf oregano
Dash black pepper
5 ounces fresh mushrooms, sliced (1-3/4 cups)

Arrange turkey evenly in a 11'' x 7'' microwave-safe dish. In a 4-cup glass measure, combine tomato sauce, wine, Worcestershire sauce, fennel seeds, oregano and pepper. Pour over turkey. Top evenly with mushrooms. Cover tightly. Microwave on 100% power (HIGH) 4 minutes. Adjust power level to 50% power (MEDIUM). Microwave 4 to 6 minutes more or until meat is no longer pink in center (cut to test). Let stand 5 minutes. Makes 4 servings.

Carbohydrate 7 g	
Protein 24.6 g	
Fat 2.8 g	

Chicken Cacciatore, atop Spaghetti Squash, page 97

Chicken Breasts with Sherry Sauce   *248 Calories*

Sherry adds flavor and minimal calories.

4 (4-oz.) boneless chicken breast halves,
  skinned
1 teaspoon browning sauce
6 ounces fresh mushrooms, sliced (2 cups)
1 tablespoon cornstarch

1/2 cup water
1/2 teaspoon browning sauce
2-1/2 tablespoons dry sherry
2 teaspoons chicken bouillon granules
1/4 cup diced green onions

Arrange chicken in a 11'' x 7'' microwave-safe dish with thickest parts to outside of dish. Brush 1 teaspoon browning sauce over both sides of chicken. Cover with wax paper. Microwave on 100% power (HIGH) 3 minutes. Rearrange, moving outside pieces to center of dish. Microwave on 100% power (HIGH) 2 to 3 minutes more or until meat in thickest part is no longer pink (cut to test). Set aside. Place mushrooms in a 4-cup glass measure. Cover tightly. Microwave on 100% power (HIGH) 1-1/2 minutes. In a small bowl, dissolve cornstarch in water. Stir in 1/2 teaspoon browning sauce, sherry, bouillon granules and green onions. Stir mixture into mushrooms. Microwave on 100% power (HIGH) 2 to 3 minutes or until slightly thickened, stirring every minute during cooking. Pour sauce over chicken. Adjust power level to 70% power (MEDIUM-HIGH). Microwave 2 to 3 minutes or until heated through. Makes 4 servings.

Carbohydrate 6.0 g	
Protein 38.4 g	
Fat 5.9 g	

How to Make Chicken Véronique Salad

1/Cooked chicken is easiest to bone and cut in cubes if done when poultry is just cool enough to handle.

2/Celery, seedless grapes and yogurt dressing are added to the chicken. Mound on a bed of fresh spinach leaves and sprinkle with almonds.

Chicken Véronique Salad

184 Calories

Pretty as a picture with flavor to match.

1-1/2 pounds boneless chicken breasts, skinned
3/4 cup diced celery
3/4 cup halved green seedless grapes
1/3 cup plain low-fat yogurt
1 tablespoon lemon juice
1/2 teaspoon curry powder
1/4 teaspoon garlic powder
Spinach leaves
2 tablespoons slivered almonds

Arrange chicken in a 9-inch microwave-safe pie plate with thickest parts to outside of pie plate. Cover with wax paper. Microwave on 100% power (HIGH) 4 minutes. Rearrange, moving outside pieces to center of dish. Microwave on 100% power (HIGH) 3 to 5 minutes more or until chicken is no longer pink in the thickest part (cut to test). Cool; remove bones. Cut in 1/2-inch chunks. In a medium bowl, combine chicken, celery, grapes, yogurt, lemon juice, curry powder and garlic powder. Arrange spinach leaves attractively on a serving plate; spoon chicken salad on spinach leaves. Sprinkle with almonds. Makes 6 servings.

Carbohydrate 5.9 g	
Protein 28.4 g	
Fat 4.7 g	

Lemony Chicken

Zesty lemon flavor with great eye appeal.

1 pound chicken pieces, skinned
1/2 teaspoon onion powder
1/2 teaspoon dried leaf thyme,
   crumbled
1/2 teaspoon dried leaf marjoram,
   crumbled

1 teaspoon lemon pepper
2 teaspoons grated lemon peel
2 tablespoons lemon juice
1-1/2 teaspoons browning sauce
2 tablespoons chopped fresh parsley

Arrange chicken on a microwave-safe rack set in a 13'' x 9'' microwave-safe dish with thickest parts to outside of dish. In a small bowl, combine onion powder, thyme, marjoram, lemon pepper, lemon peel, lemon juice and browning sauce. Brush mixture over both sides of chicken. Cover with wax paper. Microwave on 100% power (HIGH) 4 minutes. Baste chicken. Rearrange, moving outside pieces to center of dish. Recover; microwave on 100% power (HIGH) 3 to 5 minutes more or until chicken is no longer pink in thickest part (cut to test), basting 2 times during cooking. Sprinkle with parsley. Makes 4 servings.

Carbohydrate 2.1 g	
Protein 27.1 g	
Fat 3.2 g	

Tip

Skinning chicken pieces results in a savings of about 20-calories per piece. Four ounces of chicken or turkey is about 220 calories without skin.

How to Make Cornish Hens with Brown Rice

1/Halved Cornish hens are arranged atop partially-cooked rice and lightly brushed with a mixture of melted margarine and browning sauce.

2/Shield wing tips and leg ends with small pieces of foil to prevent them from over-cooking.

Cornish Hens with Brown Rice

648 Calories

Serve with vegetables for a complete dinner. These are large portions of meat. For smaller servings, one pound game hens are available by special order.

1-1/4 cups water
1 garlic clove, minced
1 cup quick-cooking brown rice
1/2 teaspoon dried leaf basil

2 (22-oz.) Rock Cornish game hens, thawed if frozen
2 teaspoons margarine
1-1/2 tablespoons browning sauce

In a shallow 2-quart microwave-safe dish, microwave water and garlic on 100% power (HIGH) 4 to 5 minutes or until boiling. Stir in rice and basil. Cover tightly. Adjust power level to 50% power (MEDIUM). Microwave 8 to 10 minutes or until liquid is almost absorbed. Remove giblets from hens; split hens in 1/2 lengthwise. Arrange, cut-side down, on top of rice. In a custard cup, microwave margarine on 100% power (HIGH) 35 to 40 seconds or until melted. Stir in browning sauce; brush mixture over hens. Cover with wax paper. Microwave on 100% power (HIGH) 10 minutes. Rearrange, moving outside halves to center of dish. Shield wing tips and leg ends with foil. Recover with wax paper. Microwave on 100% power (HIGH) 6 to 8 minutes or until juices run clear when birds are cut between breast and thigh. Let stand covered 5 minutes. Makes 4 servings.

Carbohydrate 28.9 g	
Protein 40.9 g	
Fat 36.8 g	

Fiesta Chicken

Finger-licking good, with a south-of-the-border taste.

1 egg white
1 cup crushed cheese-flavored crackers
  (about 20 (1-inch round) crackers)

2 tablespoons chili powder
1 pound chicken pieces, skinned

In a small bowl, beat egg white. In a pie plate, combine crackers and chili powder. Dip each piece of chicken in egg white. Roll in crumb mixture to coat. Place in a shallow microwave-safe dish with thickest parts to outside of dish. Microwave on 100% power (HIGH) 4 minutes. Rearrange, moving outside pieces to center of dish. Microwave on 100% power (HIGH) 3 to 4 minutes more or until meat in thickest part is no longer pink (cut to test). Makes 4 servings.

Carbohydrate 5.4 g	
Protein 26.5 g	
Fat 8.1 g	

Broccoli-Stuffed Chicken

Prepare this dish in the morning before work; serve to dinner guests with a minimum of time and effort.

1/2 pound fresh broccoli, cut in 8 spears
4 (4-oz.) boneless chicken breast halves,
  skinned, pounded 1/4-inch thick

1 tablespoon margarine
1-1/2 teaspoons browning sauce

Peel stalk of each broccoli spear. In a shallow microwave-safe dish, arrange broccoli with stalks to outside of dish. Cover tightly. Microwave on 100% power (HIGH) 2 minutes. Place 2 broccoli spears on each chicken breast half. Roll up; secure with wooden picks. Place chicken rolls in an 8-inch microwave-safe dish; set aside. In a 1-cup glass measure, microwave margarine on 100% power (HIGH) 45 to 50 seconds or until melted. Stir in browning sauce. Brush mixture over both sides of chicken. Cover with wax paper. Microwave on 100% power (HIGH) 6 to 8 minutes or until chicken is no longer pink in center (cut to test). Makes 4 servings.

Carbohydrate 3.1 g	
Protein 28.9 g	
Fat 6.7 g	

Texas Turkey Hash

235 Calories

Canned tomatoes provide moisture for rice to cook.

1 pound ground turkey
1 large onion, chopped
1 green bell pepper, chopped
1 (16-oz.) can tomatoes

1/2 cup long-grain white rice
1 teaspoon chili powder
1/2 teaspoon salt
1/8 teaspoon black pepper

In a microwave-safe plastic colander, combine turkey, onion and bell pepper. Set colander in a microwave-safe bowl. Microwave on 100% power (HIGH) 5 to 6 minutes or until meat is no longer pink, stirring several times with a fork during cooking. In a 2-quart microwave-safe casserole dish, combine turkey mixture, tomatoes with juice, rice, chili powder, salt and black pepper. Cover tightly. Microwave on 100% power (HIGH) 15 to 18 minutes or until rice is tender, stirring 2 times during cooking. Let stand 10 minutes. Makes 4 servings.

Carbohydrate 17.9 g	
Protein 24.8 g	
Fat 6.7 g	

Turkey Macaroni

261 Calories

High nutrition on a shoestring budget.

1 pound ground turkey
1/2 cup chopped onion
1/2 cup chopped green bell pepper
1 (15-oz.) can unsalted tomato sauce
1/2 cup water

1 cup uncooked elbow macaroni
1 teaspoon Italian herb seasoning
1/4 cup shredded sharp Cheddar cheese (1 oz.)

In a microwave-safe plastic colander, combine turkey, onion and bell pepper. Set colander in a microwave-safe bowl. Microwave on 100% power (HIGH) 5 to 6 minutes or until meat is no longer pink, stirring several times with a fork during cooking. In a 2-quart microwave-safe casserole, combine turkey mixture, tomato sauce, water, macaroni and herb seasoning. Cover tightly. Microwave on 100% power (HIGH) 13 to 15 minutes or until macaroni is tender, stirring several times during cooking. Sprinkle with cheese. Let stand 5 minutes. Makes 4 servings.

Carbohydrate 18.8 g	
Protein 27.2 g	
Fat 8.4 g	

Fish & Shellfish

The average American consumes less than 14 pounds of seafood a year, compared to about 150 pounds of red meat. But the tide is turning in favor of seafood. The latest medical research shows that fish, especially fattier types such as salmon, mackerel and trout, contain a high concentration of a polyunsaturated fat called *omega 3*. This fatty acid lowers blood cholesterol levels, actually decreasing the risk of heart disease. No studies have precisely determined the minimum or maximum daily consumption of fish oils desirable for good health, but dietitians suggests that a healthful diet should include fish at least twice a week. Shellfish, too, is a valuable addition to the diet; though it isn't high in omega 3, it's rich in protein and low in fat.

If you haven't eaten much seafood before, now is the time to learn creative, delicious ways to serve it. Always begin with fresh fish and shellfish. Fresh fish should have firm, moist flesh and bright, shiny skin; whole fish should have clear, protruding eyes. The aroma should *never* be fishy. Frozen fish is a good buy; make sure it's free of ice crystals and signs of freezer burn.

Most shellfish are sold in several different forms: fresh (live or cooked), frozen, and/or canned and ready to use. Shrimp are available year 'round—fresh or frozen, in the shell or shelled and deveined. Good quality shrimp are moist to the touch, with a fresh, slightly sweet aroma. Scallops, too, are available fresh or frozen; like shrimp, they should smell slightly sweet. If you're purchasing scallops already packaged, choose a package with little or no liquid in the bottom.

Both fish and shellfish are highly perishable. Refrigerate promptly after purchase and use within 24 hours—or better yet, on the day of purchase. Use thawed frozen seafood right away. Never refreeze a completely or partially thawed fish.

The nutritious microwave recipes in this chapter offer a perfect way to add seafood to your eating plan. Even those who don't like seafood will be won over by sauced dishes such as Shrimp-Stuffed Sole, Salmon Patties and Fish Véronique.

One caution applies to all these recipes, though: *don't overcook*. Over-microwaved fish is dry, tough and rubbery. For moist, tender seafood, microwave *just* until it turns from translucent to opaque and begins to flake when a fork is inserted in the thickest part. Microwave shrimp *just* until they turn pink.

Clam Chowder

To assure even cooking, cut vegetables in uniform pieces. Serve with a crisp green salad to make this hearty meal complete.

2 teaspoons margarine
1 large carrot, finely chopped
   (1/2 cup)
1 medium onion, finely chopped
   (1 cup)
1 (8-oz.) potato, peeled,
   finely chopped

2 tablespoons all-purpose flour
2 cups skim milk
1 (6-1/2-oz.) can minced clams
1/8 teaspoon white pepper
1 tablespoon minced fresh parsley
Salt to taste

In a large deep microwave-safe bowl, microwave margarine on 100% power (HIGH) 20 seconds or until melted. Stir in carrot, onion and potato. Cover tightly. Microwave on 100% power (HIGH) 5 minutes. Stir; recover. Microwave on 100% power (HIGH) 6 minutes more or until vegetables are tender. Stir in flour. Microwave on 100% power (HIGH) 1 minute or until bubbly. Gradually stir in milk. Drain clam juice into vegetables; set clams aside. Stir in pepper. Recover; microwave on 100% power (HIGH) 5 minutes. Stir; recover. Microwave on 100% power (HIGH) 2 minutes or until bubbly and thickened. Stir in reserved clams and parsley. Salt to taste. Make 4 (1-cup) servings.

Carbohydrate 34.2 g	
Protein 34.6 g	
Fat 3.8 g	

Fish Fillets with Garlic-Lime Sauce

Lime juice adds the flavor—there's no salt added! Serve with brown rice and peas for a colorful meal.

4 (4-oz.) white fish fillets, about 1 inch thick,
1/2 cup diced onion
2 teaspoons lime juice
1 tablespoon margarine

1 garlic clove, minced
1/2 teaspoon grated lime peel
Lime slices

Arrange fish in a shallow microwave-safe dish with thickest parts to outside of dish. Sprinkle with onion. Cover with wax paper. Microwave on 100% power (HIGH) 2 minutes. Rearrange, moving outside pieces to center of dish. Recover; microwave on 100% power (HIGH) 1 to 3 minutes more or until fish turns opaque and just begins to flake when a fork is inserted in thickest part. Set aside. In a custard cup, combine lime juice, margarine, garlic and lime peel. Microwave on 100% power (HIGH) 1 minute. Pour evenly over fish. Garnish with lime slices. Makes 4 servings.

Carbohydrate 2 g	
Protein 23 g	
Fat 4 g	

Shrimp-Stuffed Sole

A sophisticated entrée for special friends. Photo on page 5.

6 (3-1/2-oz.) sole fillets, 1/4 inch thick
1/3 pound small cooked shrimp
1/2 cup dry white wine
3 tablespoons margarine
3 tablespoons minced onion
3 ounces fresh mushrooms, sliced (1 cup)

1-1/2 tablespoons all-purpose flour
1/2 cup skim milk
Paprika to taste
3/4 pound spinach, washed, coarsely chopped
Small parsley sprigs

Top sole fillets evenly with shrimp; roll up fillets jelly-roll style. Place fish rolls, seam-side down, in a shallow microwave-safe dish. Pour wine over fish. Cover tightly. Microwave on 100% power (HIGH) 3 minutes. Rearrange, moving outside rolls to center of dish. Recover; microwave on 100% power (HIGH) 1 to 2 minutes more or until fish turns opaque and just begins to flake when a fork is inserted in thickest part. Drain liquid; reserve 1/4 cup. Recover. In a 2-cup glass measure, combine margarine, onion and mushrooms. Microwave on 100% power (HIGH) 2 minutes. Stir in flour. Microwave on 100% power (HIGH) 1 minute or until bubbly. Gradually stir in milk. Microwave on 100% power (HIGH) 2 to 3 minutes or until thickened. Stir in reserved 1/4 cup fish liquid. Arrange spinach on a microwave-safe platter. Place fish rolls on spinach. Sprinkle each fish roll with paprika. Top with sauce. Microwave on 100% power (HIGH) 1 minute, if desired. Garnish with parsley sprigs. Makes 6 servings.

Carbohydrate 4.4 g	
Protein 23.5 g	
Fat 7.2 g	

Tip

For high nutrition, good taste and fast microwave cooking, fish is hard to beat. It's high in vitamins, low in fat and provides potassium, phosphorus, iron, iodine, fluoride and zinc. A 3-1/2 ounce serving of lean fish (such as sole or flounder) has under 100 calories.

How to Make "French-Fried" Scallops

1/Scallops are dipped in oil-free Italian dressing, then into seasoned, whole-wheat bread crumb mixture.

2/Looking as though they were deep-fried, the calorie-pared, microwaved scallops are garnished with lemon and parsley

"French-Fried" Scallops

152 Calories

Enjoy that French-fried flavor without the fat.

1 pound fresh or thawed frozen sea scallops
1/2 cup oil-free Italian salad dressing
1/3 cup fine dry whole-wheat bread crumbs
1/3 cup grated Parmesan cheese

1/2 teaspoon paprika
Lemon wedges
Parsley sprigs

Rinse scallops; pat very dry with paper towels. Pour dressing into a shallow bowl. In a pie plate, combine bread crumbs, cheese and paprika. Dip scallops in dressing; roll in crumb mixture to coat well. Arrange scallops, in a circle, on a microwave-safe plate. Microwave on 100% power (HIGH) 2 minutes. Rearrange, moving outside pieces to center of dish. Microwave on 100% power (HIGH) 1 to 2 minutes more or *just* until scallops are firm (test with knife). Garnish with lemon wedges and parsley sprigs. Makes 4 servings.

Carbohydrate 9.7 g	
Protein 19 g	
Fat 3.5 g	

Skinny Shrimp Scampi

177 Calories

At 7 grams protein, 0.7 grams fat and just 33 calories per ounce, shrimp is a nutritional bargain.

2 tablespoons margarine
2 tablespoons lemon juice
2 garlic cloves, minced
1/2 teaspoon butter-flavored salt

1/8 teaspoon black pepper
1 pound uncooked large shrimp,
  shelled, deveined (about 18 to 20)
1 tablespoon minced fresh parsley

In a shallow 1-1/2-quart microwave-safe dish, microwave margarine on 100% power (HIGH) 55 to 60 seconds or until melted. Stir in lemon juice, garlic, butter-flavored salt and pepper. Stir in shrimp. Microwave on 100% power (HIGH) 1-1/2 minutes. Rearrange, moving outside shrimp to center of dish. Microwave on 100% power (HIGH) 1-1/2 minutes more or *just* until shrimp turn pink. Sprinkle with parsley. Makes 4 servings.

Carbohydrate 1.9 g	
Protein 27.6 g	
Fat 6.2 g	

Shrimp Kabobs

129 Calories

Serve these kabobs for a summer party.

1 medium, green bell pepper, seeded,
  cut in 12 pieces
2 small onions, each cut in 6 wedges
12 medium mushrooms
12 cherry tomatoes, stemmed
1 pound uncooked large shrimp,
  shelled, deveined (about 18 to 20)

1/4 cup lite soy sauce
1/2 cup dry white wine
1 teaspoon sugar
1/2 teasoon garlic powder
1/2 teaspoon ground ginger

Combine bell pepper, onion, mushrooms, tomatoes and shrimp in bowl. In a 2-cup glass measure, combine soy sauce, wine, sugar, garlic and ginger. Pour over vegetable-shrimp mixture. Cover tightly. Refrigerate several hours, stirring once or twice. Thread vegetables and shrimp on 6 wooden skewers. Arrange in a 13'' x 9'' microwave-safe dish. Cover with wax paper. Microwave on 50% power (MEDIUM) 8 minutes. Rearrange, moving outside skewers to center of dish. Baste; recover. Microwave on 50% power (MEDIUM) 8 minutes more or *just* until shrimp turn pink and bell pepper is tender. Makes 6 servings.

Carbohydrate 6.6 g	
Protein 19.6 g	
Fat 2 g	

Skinny Shrimp Scampi, Vegetable Medley, page 96

Coquilles St. Jacques

210 Calories

A rich yet low-calorie version of an elegant classic.

1 pound fresh or thawed frozen sea scallops
1 tablespoon margarine
1-1/2 cups sliced fresh mushrooms
1/2 cup diced green onions
1/3 cup dry white wine
2 teaspoons lemon juice
2 tablespoons all-purpose flour

1/8 teaspoon ground nutmeg
1/3 cup skim milk
1/4 cup diced Swiss-style low-fat processed cheese product (1 oz.)
2 tablespoons soft bread crumbs
1 tablespoon chopped fresh parsley

Rinse scallops; pat dry with paper towels. In a 1-1/2-quart microwave-safe casserole dish, microwave margarine on 100% power (HIGH) 45 to 50 seconds or until melted. Stir in scallops, mushrooms, green onions, wine and lemon juice. Adjust power level to 50% power (MEDIUM). Microwave 7 to 10 minutes or *just* until scallops turn from translucent to opaque, stirring several times during cooking. Using a slotted spoon, remove scallops and mushrooms to a plate. Stir flour and nutmeg into juices. Microwave on 100% power (HIGH) 1 minute or until bubbly. Gradually stir in milk until smooth. Microwave on 100% power (HIGH) 1 to 2 minutes or until thickened. Stir in cheese and scallop-mushroom mixture. Sprinkle with bread crumbs. Microwave on 100% power (HIGH) 1 minute or until heated through. Sprinkle with parsley. Makes 4 servings.

Carbohydrate 14.4 g	
Protein 23.7 g	
Fat 5.4 g	

Microwave "Fried" Fish

113 Calories

Crispy fried flavor minus the fat.

1/3 cup cornflake crumbs
1 tablespoon chopped fresh parsley
1/2 teaspoon paprika

4 (4-oz.) flounder fillets, about 3/4 inch thick
2 tablespoons calorie-reduced mayonnaise

In a pie plate, combine cornflake crumbs, parsley and paprika. Spread both sides of each fish fillet evenly with mayonnaise. Coat both sides of fillets with crumb mixture. Arrange fish, in a single layer, in a microwave-safe dish with thickest parts to outside of dish. Microwave on 100% power (HIGH) 2 minutes. Rearrange, moving outside pieces to center of dish. Microwave on 100% power (HIGH) 2 to 3 minutes more or until fish turns opaque and just begins to flake when a fork is inserted in thickest part. Makes 4 servings.

Carbohydrate 2 g	
Protein 19.4 g	
Fat 2.9 g	

Polynesian Fish

147 Calories

Pineapple gives this fish sweet flavor; tomato and bell pepper add color appeal.

4 (4-oz.) sole fillets, 1/4 inch thick
2 teaspoons lite soy sauce
1 tablespoon lemon juice
1/4 teaspoon ground ginger
1 (8-oz.) can crushed pineapple
  packed in unsweetened pineapple
  juice, drained

1 medium green bell pepper, seeded,
  cut in strips
1 medium tomato, cut in wedges

Arrange fish in a single layer in a shallow microwave-safe dish with thickest parts to outside of dish. Sprinkle with soy sauce, lemon juice and ginger. Top with pineapple, bell pepper and tomato. Cover with wax paper. Microwave on 100% power (HIGH) 3 minutes. Rearrange, moving outside pieces to center of dish. Microwave on 100% power (HIGH) 1 to 2 minutes more or until fish turns opaque and just begins to flake when a fork is inserted in thickest part. Makes 4 servings.

Carbohydrate 8 g	
Protein 24.6 g	
Fat 1.5 g	

Colorful Baked Perch

112 Calories

Red bell peppers give this dish delicious flavor (they're sweeter than green bell peppers).

4 (4-oz.) perch fillets, 1/2 inch thick
1/4 teaspoon garlic powder
1/4 teaspoon black pepper

1-1/2 ounces fresh mushrooms, sliced (1/2 cup)
1/4 cup diced red bell pepper
1/4 cup chopped green onions

Arrange fish in a single layer in a shallow microwave-safe dish with thickest parts to outside of dish. Sprinkle with garlic powder and black pepper. Top evenly with mushrooms, bell pepper and green onions. Cover with wax paper. Microwave on 100% power (HIGH) 3 minutes. Rearrange, moving outside pieces to center of dish. Microwave on 100% power (HIGH) 1 to 2 minutes more or until fish turns opaque and just begins to flake when a fork is inserted in thickest part. Makes 4 servings.

Carbohydrate 1.4 g	
Protein 22.9 g	
Fat 1.4 g	

Salmon with Lemon Sauce

252 Calories

A simple—and simply delicious—lunch or dinner offering. Photo on cover.

4 (4-oz.) salmon steaks
4 lemon slices
1 teaspoon cornstarch
1/3 cup chicken broth

1 teaspoon lemon juice
1/2 teaspoon grated lemon peel
1/2 teaspoon minced fresh chives
Dash white pepper

Arrange steaks in a shallow microwave-safe dish with thickest parts to outside of dish. Place a lemon slice on each steak. Cover tightly. Microwave salmon on 70% power (MEDIUM-HIGH) 2 minutes. Rearrange, moving outside steaks to center of dish. Recover; microwave on 70% power (MEDIUM-HIGH) 1 to 2 minutes more or until fish just turns opaque. Let stand covered 5 minutes. To make sauce, in a 1-cup glass measure, dissolve cornstarch in chicken broth. Microwave on 70% power (MEDIUM-HIGH) 1-1/2 to 2 minutes or until sauce comes to a boil and is clear and thickened, stirring several times during cooking. Stir in lemon juice, lemon peel and chives. Using a spatula, carefully transfer salmon to heated plates. Spoon sauce over each steak. Sprinkle with pepper. Makes 4 servings.

Carbohydrate 0.8 g	
Protein 20.2 g	
Fat 13.4 g	

Tartar Sauce

18 Calories/tablespoon

A favorite accompaniment for fish . . . especially this low-fat version.

2/3 cup plain low-fat yogurt
1/3 cup calorie-reduced mayonnaise

2 tablespoons sweet pickle relish
1/2 teaspoon onion powder

In a small bowl, combine yogurt, mayonnaise, pickle relish and onion powder. Cover tightly. Refrigerate several hours to allow flavors to blend. Makes about 1 cup.

Carbohydrate 2.0 g	
Protein .5 g	
Fat 1.0 g	

How to Make Apricot Shrimp Curry

1/To devein shrimp, remove shells, then remove sand vein by making a shallow cut down back of each shrimp. Lift out vein with tip of knife.

2/Add shrimp to well-seasoned, bouillon-based sauce and cook *just* until they turn pink, bringing uncooked shrimp in center to outside of dish halfway through cooking.

Apricot Shrimp Curry

235 Calories

A low-fat choice for the health-conscious diner.

1 tablespoon margarine
1 cup chopped onion
1-1/2 tablespoons cornstarch
1 (10-1/2-oz.) can condensed beef
   broth (bouillon)
1 (16-oz.) can apricot halves packed
   in juice, drained, chopped

1 teaspoon curry powder
1/4 teaspoon ground ginger
Dash red (cayenne) pepper
2 tablespoons lemon juice
1 pound uncooked medium shrimp,
   shelled, deveined (30 to 40)
3 cups hot, cooked rice

In a shallow 2-quart microwave-safe casserole dish, combine margarine and onion. Cover tightly. Microwave on 100% power (HIGH) 1-1/2 minutes. In a small bowl, stir cornstarch into beef broth until dissolved. Add to onions. Stir in apricots, curry powder, ginger, red pepper and lemon juice. Microwave on 100% power (HIGH) 5 to 6 minutes or until thickened, stirring every minute during cooking. Stir in shrimp. Microwave on 100% power (HIGH) 2 minutes. Rearrange, moving outside shrimp to center of dish. Microwave 1 to 2 minutes more or *just* until shrimp turn pink. Serve over rice. Makes 6 servings.

Carbohydrate 30.8 g	
Protein 21.7 g	
Fat 2.3 g	

Tuna Taters

Surprise the family with this tasty protein-fiber combination.

4 (5- to 5-1/2 oz.) baking potatoes,
  scrubbed, pierced
1/4 cup skim milk
1/2 teaspoon garlic salt
1 (6-1/2-oz.) can white tuna packed
  in water, drained

1/4 cup minced green onions
1/4 cup shredded Cheddar cheese (1 oz.)
2 tablespoons sliced ripe olives
4 cherry tomatoes, cut in halves

Line bottom of microwave oven with a paper towel. Place potatoes on paper towel. Microwave on 100% power (HIGH) 5 minutes. Turn over. Microwave on 100% power (HIGH) 5 to 7 minutes more or until *just* soft when squeezed. Cool. Cut a slice off top of each potato. Scoop out pulp into a large bowl, leaving a 1/4-inch-thick shell. Set shells aside. Combine pulp, milk, garlic salt, tuna and green onions; mix well. Fill potato shells with mixture. Sprinkle with cheese. Arrange potatoes spoke-fashion on a microwave-safe plate. Microwave on 100% power (HIGH) 3 to 4 minutes or until potatoes are heated through. Garnish with olives and tomatoes. Makes 4 servings.

Carbohydrate 35 g	
Protein 19.7 g	
Fat 5 g	

Creamy Tuna

Tuna is a staple you should always keep on hand for quick meals.

1 tablespoon margarine
1 tablespoon all-purpose flour
1-1/3 cups skim milk
Dash white pepper
1/4 teaspoon dried dill weed
1 (6-1/2-oz.) can white tuna packed in
  water, drained, flaked

1 teaspoon lemon juice
1/2 cup frozen green peas
2 cups hot, cooked rice
2 teaspoons chopped pimentos, drained
  (1-1/3 oz.)

In a 4-cup glass measure, microwave margarine on 100% power (HIGH) 45 to 50 seconds or until melted. Stir in flour. Microwave on 100% power (HIGH) 1 minute or until bubbly. Gradually stir in milk, pepper and dill weed. Microwave on 100% power (HIGH) 3 to 4 minutes or until thickened, stirring every minute during cooking. Stir in tuna. Microwave on 100% power (HIGH) 3 minutes, stirring every minute during cooking. Stir in peas and lemon juice. Serve with rice. Sprinkle with pimentos. Makes 4 servings.

Carbohydrate 33.2 g	
Protein 19.2 g	
Fat 3.9 g	

How to Make Surprise Sole Rolls

1/Spread spinach filling down center of each sole fillet, leaving a 1/4-inch border. Roll up, jelly-roll style, and arrange in microwave-safe dish.

2/Sole is cooked until it turns opaque and just begins to flake when a fork is inserted in center.

Surprise Sole Rolls

112 Calories

A perfect company dish: tender sole with a savory spinach stuffing.

1 (10-oz.) package frozen chopped
   spinach
3/4 cup plain low-fat yogurt
1 tablespoon cornstarch
1/2 cup chopped green onions

1-1/2 teaspoons lemon juice
1/2 teaspoon garlic powder
6 (4-oz.) sole fillets
Paprika to taste

Remove wrapper from spinach package. Place in a microwave-safe bowl. Microwave on 100% power (HIGH) 7 minutes. Drain well; press out all water. In a medium microwave-safe bowl, combine spinach, yogurt, cornstarch, green onions, lemon juice and garlic powder. Microwave on 100% power (HIGH) 1-1/2 to 2 minutes. Spread mixture down middle of each fillet to 1/4 inch of edges. Roll up fillets jelly roll-style. Secure each with a wooden pick. Arrange fish rolls in an 11'' x 7'' microwave-safe dish. Sprinkle with paprika. Microwave on 100% power (HIGH) 3 minutes. Rearrange, moving outside rolls to center of dish. Microwave on 100% power (HIGH) 2 to 3 minutes more or until fish turns opaque and just begins to flake when a fork is inserted in center. Makes 6 servings.

Carbohydrate 5.6 g	
Protein 18.8 g	
Fat 1.2 g	

Salmon Patties with Cheese Sauce *281 Calories*

Canned salmon, if eaten complete with bones, is an excellent source of calcium.

1 (15-1/2-oz.) can pink salmon, drained
2 eggs, lightly beaten
1/2 cup chopped onion

1/2 cup soft bread crumbs
1/2 cup chopped fresh parsley
1 teaspoon dry mustard

Cheese Sauce:
1 tablespoon margarine
2 tablespoons all-purpose flour
1/8 teaspoon white pepper

3/4 cup skim milk
1/3 cup shredded sharp Cheddar
   cheese (1-1/3 oz.)

Remove and discard salmon skin and cartilage; do not remove bones. Place in a medium bowl. Flake with a fork. Mix in eggs, onion, bread crumbs, parsley and mustard. Shape into 5 (1/2-inch-thick) patties. Arrange in a circle on a microwave-safe plate. Set aside. To make Cheese Sauce, in a 2-cup glass measure, microwave margarine on 100% power (HIGH) 45 to 50 seconds or until melted. Stir in flour and pepper. Gradually stir in milk. Microwave on 100% power (HIGH) 2 to 3 minutes or until thickened, stirring every minute during cooking. Add cheese; stir until melted. Set aside. Microwave salmon patties on 100% power (HIGH) 4 minutes. Rearrange, moving outside pieces to center of dish. Microwave on 100% power (HIGH) 1 to 2 minutes more or until firm throughout but still moist (cut to test). Microwave Cheese Sauce on 100% power (HIGH) 1 minute. Pour over patties. Makes 5 servings.

Carbohydrate 10.8 g	
Protein 23.1 g	
Fat 15.8 g	

Tip

Sneak extra calcium into everyday cooking by adding instant nonfat dry milk (150 milligrams calcium per tablespoon) to recipes. Mix 2 to 4 tablespoons into casseroles, quick breads, cream soups and cookies.

Fish Véronique

An attractive dish combining fish and fresh green grapes.

3/4 cup dry white wine
1/2 cup water
1/4 cup chopped fresh parsley
1/4 cup thinly sliced green onions
1/8 teaspoon black pepper

6 (4-oz.) sole fillets, 1/4 inch thick
1 lemon, thinly sliced
2 teaspoons cornstarch
1 cup seedless green grapes
Small parsley sprigs

In a small bowl, combine wine, 1/4 cup of water, parsley, onions and pepper. Set aside. Arrange fish, in a single layer, in a microwave-safe dish with thickest parts to outside of dish. Top evenly with lemon slices. Pour wine mixture evenly over fish and lemon. Cover tightly. Microwave on 100% power (HIGH) 3 minutes. Rearrange, moving outside pieces to center of dish. Recover; microwave on 100% power (HIGH) 1 to 2 minutes more or until fish turns opaque and just begins to flake when a fork is inserted in thickest part. Transfer fish and lemon slices to a platter. Pour liquid into a 2-cup glass measure. Dissolve cornstarch in remaining 1/4 cup of water. Stir into hot liquid. Microwave on 100% power (HIGH) 2 to 3 minutes or until clear and slightly thickened, stirring every minute during cooking. Stir in grapes. Pour sauce over fish. Garnish with parsley sprigs. Makes 6 servings.

Carbohydrate 6.1 g	
Protein 34.9 g	
Fat 0.8 g	

Meats

Red meats include beef, veal, lamb and pork. In an effort to cut down on cholesterol and fat, health-conscious Americans have been eating less of these meats in recent years. But red meats are still an excellent source of protein and vitamins—and thanks to modern food technology and advances in agriculture, today's meat products are leaner than ever. Meats can be a valuable addition to your diet. Be sure to choose the leanest cuts possible, trim off all visible fat and control portion sizes carefully.

Beef is power-packed food, with a high ratio of nutrients to calories. A 4-ounce serving supplies significant amounts of protein, iron, zinc, B vitamins and other nutrients. For the very best food value, buy lean beef. Choose ground beef labeled "extra-lean." According to USDA standards, "ground beef" is about 30% fat, "ground chuck" or "lean ground beef" is about 25% fat and "ground round" or "extra-lean ground beef" is about 15% fat.

In microwaving beef, just as in conventional cooking, different techniques are suited to different cuts of meat. Tender beef is dry-roasted uncovered on a microwave rack; tougher cuts require liquid and are microwaved tightly covered at a lower power level to tenderize.

Lamb is naturally lean, as it comes from young animals which haven't had time to store fat. It provides high-quality protein plus essential vitamins and minerals.

Pork, too, has excellent nutritional value. It's especially rich in B vitamins. (Stay away from bacon, sausages and spareribs, though, as these are all high in fat.) To keep fresh pork moist, microwave in a covered dish or a cooking bag. Always cook pork until well-done (to an internal temperature of 170F, 75C) —it should no longer show any trace of pinkness.

Slim Stew

A one-dish meal that's high in iron.

1-1/2 pounds round steak,
   trimmed of excess fat, cut in 1-inch cubes
1/2 pound fresh mushrooms, sliced
4 medium carrots, peeled, sliced
2 medium onions, sliced
2 (5-1/2 oz.) baking potatoes, peeled,
   cut in cubes

1 (16-oz.) can tomatoes
1 (10-1/2-oz.) can condensed beef
   broth (bouillon)
2 tablespoons quick-cooking tapioca
1 teaspoon browning sauce
1/4 teaspoon black pepper

Place steak in a 4-quart microwave-safe dish. Cover tightly. Microwave on 70% power (MEDIUM-HIGH) 9 minutes or until no longer pink. Add mushrooms, carrots, onions, potatoes and tomatoes with juice. In a small bowl, combine beef broth, tapioca, browning sauce and pepper. Pour beef broth mixture over steak and vegetables. Mix well; recover. Adjust power level to 30% power (MEDIUM-LOW). Microwave 1-1/2 hours or until meat is tender. Let stand 10 minutes. Makes 8 servings.

Carbohydrate 21.9 g	
Protein 30.8 g	
Fat 5.5 g	

Onion Steak

Microwaving at a lower power level—like conventional gentle simmering—tenderizes round steak.

1-1/2 pounds round steak,
   trimmed of excess fat, tenderized
2 tablespoons all-purpose flour
1/2 teaspoon garlic powder

1/4 teaspoon black pepper
1 medium onion, sliced
1 cup condensed beef broth (bouillon)
1/4 cup chopped fresh parsley

Cut steaks in serving-size pieces. In a pie plate, combine flour, garlic powder and pepper. Dredge meat in flour mixture. Place in a shallow microwave-safe casserole dish. Top with onion. Pour broth over meat; sprinkle with parsley. Cover tightly. Microwave on 100% power (HIGH) 5 minutes. Adjust power level to 50% power (MEDIUM). Microwave 10 minutes. Rearrange, moving outside pieces to center of dish. Microwave 10 to 15 more minutes or until meat is fork-tender. Let stand 5 minutes. Makes 6 servings.

Carbohydrate 4.3 g	
Protein 37.2 g	
Fat 6.9 g	

Mexican Pizzas

188 Calories

Olé! Mexican spices flavor an Italian delight.

1/2 pound extra-lean ground beef
1/2 cup chopped green onions
1 large tomato, chopped
1 garlic clove, minced
1/8 teaspoon red (cayenne) pepper
1/4 teaspoon chili powder

Dash black pepper
3 whole-wheat English muffins, split, toasted
1/4 cup shredded part-skim mozzarella
    cheese (1 oz.)
1/4 cup grated Parmesan cheese
    (3/4 oz.)

In a microwave-safe plastic colander, combine beef and green onions. Set colander in a microwave-safe bowl. Microwave on 100% power (HIGH) 2 minutes. Stir with a fork. Microwave on 100% power (HIGH) 1 to 2 minutes more or until meat is no longer pink. In a medium microwave-safe bowl, combine beef mixture, tomato, garlic, red pepper, chili powder and black pepper. Microwave on 100% power (HIGH) 2 to 3 minutes or until heated through. Place muffin halves, cut-side up, in a circle, on a microwave-safe plate. Spoon beef mixture over each muffin half. Sprinkle with mozzarella cheese and Parmesan cheese. Microwave on 100% power (HIGH) 2 to 3 minutes or until cheese is melted. Makes 6 servings.

Carbohydrate 20.6 g	
Protein 13.9 g	
Fat 5.7 g	

Tip

The most expensive cuts of beef are highest in fat—so you'll save calories as well as dollars by choosing flank steak over rib steak. For your ground beef recipes, buy "extra-lean" or have your butcher grind bottom round for you. Ground round has less than 15% fat; regular ground beef contains about 30% fat.

How to Make Pepper Steak

1/Flank steak is easier to slice in thin strips if placed in the freezer for 15 minutes before cutting.

2/Meat is marinated in a spicy soy-based sauce, then cooked with onion, green pepper and mushrooms.

Pepper Steak

331 Calories

Flank steak is the leanest cut of beef. Cutting flank steak across the grain produces tender meat slices.

**3/4 pound flank steak,
   trimmed of excess fat, sliced across
   grain in 1/4-inch slices
1 tablespoon cornstarch
1/4 cup dry white wine
1/3 cup lite soy sauce
1/2 teaspoon ground ginger**

**1 garlic clove, minced
1 small onion, sliced
1 large green bell pepper, seeded,
   cut in thin strips
3 ounces fresh mushrooms, sliced (1 cup)
2 cups hot, cooked rice**

Place meat slices in a 2-quart microwave-safe casserole dish. Set aside. In a 4-cup glass measure, dissolve cornstarch in wine. Stir in soy sauce, ginger and garlic. Pour over steak; mix gently. Cover tightly; let stand 30 minutes. Stir onion into steak mixture. Recover; microwave on 100% power (HIGH) 2-1/2 minutes. Stir; recover. Microwave on 100% power (HIGH) 2-1/2 minutes more. Stir in bell pepper and mushrooms. Recover; microwave on 100% power (HIGH) 2 to 3 minutes more or until meat is done and bell pepper is tender-crisp. Serve over rice. Makes 4 servings.

Carbohydrate 34.6 g	
Protein 29.6 g	
Fat 6.6 g	

Meat & Potato Roll

Combining turkey and beef boosts the flavor of meat loaf—and cuts the fat.

2 (5-1/2-oz.) baking potatoes, peeled
1-1/2 tablespoons chopped fresh parsley
1/4 teaspoon dried leaf thyme
1/4 teaspoon dried leaf marjoram
1/2 cup chopped onion
1/2 cup chopped green bell pepper
1 pound ground turkey

1/2 pound extra-lean ground beef
1/2 cup soft bread crumbs
1 egg
1/4 cup low-sodium lite ketchup
1/2 teaspoon dry mustard
Fresh herbs, if desired
Cherry tomatoes, if desired

In a small microwave-safe bowl, sprinkle potatoes with parsley, thyme and marjoram. Cover tightly. Microwave on 100% power (HIGH) 6 to 7 minutes or until fork-tender. Coarsely mash; set aside. In a medium microwave-safe bowl, combine onion and bell pepper. Cover tightly. Microwave on 100% power (HIGH) 1 minute. Mix in turkey, beef, bread crumbs and egg. On a piece of wax paper form meat mixture into a 14'' x 8'' rectangle. Spread mashed potatoes over meat rectangle to within 2 inches of all 4 sides. Roll up meat jelly-roll style, starting with a short end; seal ends. Place in an 11'' x 7'' microwave-safe dish. Cover with wax paper. Microwave on 100% power (HIGH) 9 minutes. Adjust power level to 50% power (MEDIUM). Microwave 4 minutes. Rotate dish 1/2 turn. Microwave on 50% power (MEDIUM) 4 to 5 minutes more. In a small bowl, combine ketchup and mustard; spread over loaf. Microwave on 100% power (HIGH) 1 minute. Garnish with fresh herbs and tomatoes, if desired. Makes 6 servings.

Carbohydrate 19.6 g	
Protein 36.4 g	
Fat 7.7 g	

How to Make Meat & Potato Roll

1/Ground turkey and beef are mixed with seasonings, formed in a rectangle on wax paper and spread with a layer of mashed potatoes. With the aid of wax paper, the meat is rolled jelly-roll style into a cylinder.

2/Cooked loaf is topped with mustard-ketchup mixture and sliced crosswise to show a pinwheel design.

Sauerbraten Meatballs

277 Calories

A sweet, spicy dish inspired by the famous German pot roast.

1 pound ground veal
1/2 pound extra-lean ground beef
1 egg, lightly beaten
1/2 cup chopped onion
1/4 teaspoon black pepper
2 teaspoons cornstarch

1 cup cold water
2 tablespoons low-sodium lite ketchup
1 tablespoon packed brown sugar
1/4 teaspoon ground ginger
1/4 teaspoon ground cloves

Mix veal, beef, egg, onion and pepper. Shape into 54 (1-inch) balls. Arrange in a microwave-safe dish. Microwave on 100% power (HIGH) 3 minutes; drain. Rearrange, moving outside pieces to center. Microwave on 100% power (HIGH) 3 to 5 minutes. Drain; set aside. Dissolve cornstarch in cold water. Stir in ketchup, brown sugar, ginger and cloves. Microwave on 100% power (HIGH) 2 to 3 minutes or until thickened, stirring every minute. Pour mixture over meatballs. Microwave on 70% power (MEDIUM-HIGH) 1 to 2 minutes. Makes 6 servings.

Carbohydrate 6.2 g	
Protein 29.2 g	
Fat 14.4 g	

Chili

A soluble fiber found in dried beans and oat bran has been shown to be effective in lowering blood cholesterol.

3/4 cup chopped onion
1/2 cup chopped green bell pepper
1 cup thinly sliced celery
1 garlic clove, minced
1 pound extra-lean ground beef
1 (16-oz.) can crushed Italian-style
   tomatoes

1 (15-oz.) can kidney beans, drained,
   rinsed
1 (8-oz.) can unsalted tomato sauce
2 teaspoons chili powder
1/2 teaspoon dried leaf oregano

In a 2-quart microwave-safe casserole dish, combine onion, bell pepper, celery and garlic. Cover tightly. Microwave on 100% power (HIGH) 3 minutes. Set aside. Place beef in a microwave-safe plastic colander. Set colander in a microwave-safe bowl. Microwave on 100% power (HIGH) 5 to 6 minutes or until meat is no longer pink, stirring several times with a fork during cooking. Stir beef into onion mixture. Stir in tomatoes with juice, beans, tomato sauce, chili powder and oregano. Cover tightly. Microwave on 100% power (HIGH) 5 minutes. Uncover; adjust power level to 50% power (MEDIUM). Microwave 11 to 15 minutes more, stirring several times during cooking. Makes 6 servings.

Carbohydrate 22.5 g	
Protein 21.9 g	
Fat 7 g	

Pineapple Pork Chops

Pork is a good source of vitamin B-1 (thiamin) needed for digestion.

1 (1-oz.) package brown-gravy mix
6 (4-oz.) loin pork chops

6 canned pineapple slices packed in
   unsweetened pineapple juice, drained

Pour brown-gravy mix into a pie plate; dredge pork chops covering both sides. Place pork chops on a microwave-safe rack set in a 13'' x 9'' microwave-safe dish. Top each chop with a pineapple slice. Cover tightly. Microwave on 100% power (HIGH) 4 minutes. Adjust power level to 30% power (MEDIUM-LOW). Microwave 8 minutes. Rearrange, moving outside pieces to center of dish. Microwave 7 to 12 minutes more or until meat is no longer pink in center (cut to test). Makes 6 servings.

Carbohydrate 7.1 g	
Protein 22.6 g	
Fat 10.8 g	

Moussaka

234 Calories

This eggplant-beef entree is a fat-reduced version of the popular Greek dish.

1 pound extra-lean ground beef	1 garlic clove, minced
1/2 cup chopped onion	1/2 teaspoon dried leaf oregano
1 (8-oz.) can tomatoes	1/4 teaspoon ground cinnamon
6 ounces fresh mushrooms, sliced (2 cups)	1 (8-oz.) package Neufchâtel cheese
1 medium eggplant, cubed (4 cups)	2 eggs
1/4 cup chopped fresh parsley	8 ounces plain low-fat yogurt (1 cup)

In a microwave-safe plastic colander, combine beef and onion. Set colander in a microwave-safe bowl. Microwave on 100% power (HIGH) 5 to 6 minutes or until beef is no longer pink, stirring several times with a fork during cooking. Set aside. Drain tomatoes, reserving juice; cut up tomatoes. In a 3-quart microwave-safe casserole dish, combine beef mixture, tomatoes and reserved juice, mushrooms, eggplant, parsley, garlic, oregano and cinnamon. Cover tightly. Adjust power level to 70% power (MEDIUM-HIGH). Microwave 25 to 30 minutes or until eggplant is tender, stirring several times during cooking. Set aside. Adjust power level to 30% power (MEDIUM-HIGH). In a small microwave-safe bowl, microwave cheese 1-1/2 minutes or until softened. Beat in eggs and yogurt. Spread over meat mixture. Adjust power level to 50% power (MEDIUM). Microwave 5 to 7 minutes or until topping is set. Makes 8 servings.

Carbohydrate 9.5 g	
Protein 19 g	
Fat 13.6 g	

Hamburger Stroganoff

331 Calories

A good family dinner and a budget booster, too.

1 pound extra-lean ground beef	1/2 cup plain low-fat yogurt
2/3 cup diced onion	2 tablespoons chopped fresh parsley
6 ounces fresh mushrooms, sliced (2 cups)	2 cups hot, cooked rice
1 (10-3/4-oz.) can condensed cream of mushroom soup	

In a microwave-safe plastic colander, combine beef and onion. Set colander in a microwave-safe bowl. Microwave on 100% power (HIGH) 5 to 6 minutes or until beef is no longer pink, stirring several times with a fork during cooking. In a 2-1/2-quart microwave-safe casserole dish, combine beef mixture, mushrooms and soup. Cover tightly. Microwave on 100% power (HIGH) 3 to 4 minutes or until flavors are blended. Stir in yogurt and parsley. Serve over rice. Makes 4 servings.

Carbohydrate 34.1 g	
Protein 23.1 g	
Fat 10.9 g	

Marvelous Meat Loaf Dinner

287 Calories

A complete dinner in under 20 minutes.

1 pound extra-lean ground beef
1/3 cup quick-cooking rolled oats
1/4 cup chopped onion
1/4 cup low-sodium lite ketchup
1 egg, lightly beaten
1/8 teaspoon black pepper

4 (2-1/2-oz.) red thin-skinned potatoes
   scrubbed, pierced
1 tablespoon packed brown sugar
1 tablespoon low-sodium lite ketchup
1/4 teaspoon dry mustard

In a medium bowl, thoroughly mix beef, oats, onion, 1/4 cup ketchup, egg and pepper. Form into a round loaf. Place on a microwave-safe rack set in a 2-1/2-quart microwave-safe casserole dish. Arrange potatoes around meat loaf. Cover with wax paper. Microwave on 100% power (HIGH) 7 minutes. Rotate dish 1/2 turn. Microwave on 100% power (HIGH) 8 to 9 minutes more or until meat loaf is no longer pink in center. In a small bowl, combine brown sugar, 1 tablespoon ketchup and mustard. Spread mixture over meat loaf. Microwave on 100% power (HIGH) 1 minute. Makes 4 servings.

Carbohydrate 18.8 g	
Protein 26.6 g	
Fat 11.3 g	

Veal Romanoff

363 Calories

Delicate-flavored, tender veal is a leaner choice than beef.

1 pound veal cuttlets, pounded 1/4-inch thick
1 medium onion, sliced
2 teaspoons cornstarch
1/3 cup dry white wine
1 (8-oz.) can unsalted tomato sauce

1 teaspoon dry mustard
1/2 cup plain low-fat yogurt
1/4 cup grated Romano cheese
   (3/4 oz.)
1/4 cup chopped fresh parsley

Arrange veal in a single layer in a 11'' x 7'' microwave-safe dish. Top with onion; set aside. In a 4-cup glass measure, dissolve cornstarch in wine. Stir in tomato sauce and mustard. Microwave on 100% power (HIGH) 2 to 3 minutes or until thickened, stirring every minute during cooking. Stir in yogurt and cheese; pour over veal. Cover tightly. Adjust power level to 50% power (MEDIUM). Microwave 6 minutes. Rearrange moving outside pieces to center of dish. Recover; microwave on 50% power (MEDIUM) 4 to 8 minutes more or until veal is tender. Sprinkle with parsley. Makes 4 servings.

Carbohydrate 10.8 g	
Protein 27.7 g	
Fat 14.9 g	

Meatza Pies

Italian flavor in minutes.

1 pound extra-lean ground beef
1 egg, lightly beaten
2 tablespoons fine dry bread crumbs
1 garlic clove, minced
1/8 teaspoon black pepper
1/2 (6-oz.) can tomato paste
  (5 tablespoons)

3 tablespoons diced onion
1/4 teaspoon dried leaf basil
1/4 teaspoon dried leaf oregano
1-1/2 ounces fresh mushrooms, sliced (1/2 cup)
1/2 cup shredded part-skim mozzarella
  cheese (2 oz.)

In a medium bowl, thoroughly mix beef, egg, bread crumbs, garlic and pepper. Form meat mixture in 4 patties, each about 3 inches in diameter. Evenly indent center of each patty forming a 1/2-inch rim around edge. Arrange patties in a 9-inch microwave-safe pie plate. In a small bowl, combine tomato paste, onion, basil and oregano. Spoon mixture evenly into center of each patty, spreading to rim. Top with mushrooms and cheese. Microwave on 100% power (HIGH) 7 to 8 minutes for medium or until meat is done to your liking. Makes 4 servings.

Carbohydrate 8.9 g	
Protein 34.1 g	
Fat 16.3 g	

Cranberry-Glazed Ham Slice

Ham is the leanest cut of pork.

3/4 cup fresh or frozen cranberries
2 teaspoons cornstarch
1/2 cup unsweetened apple juice

2 tablespoons packed light brown sugar
1 (1-lb.) fully-cooked ham slice,
  1/2 inch thick

Place cranberries in a 4-cup glass measure. Cover tightly. Microwave on 100% power (HIGH) 2 minutes (3 minutes if using frozen cranberries). In a small bowl, dissolve cornstarch in apple juice. Stir apple juice mixture and brown sugar into cranberries. Microwave on 100% power (HIGH) 2 to 3 minutes or until thickened, stirring every minute during cooking. Set aside. Place ham slice in a 12'' x 8'' microwave-safe dish. Cover with wax paper. Adjust power level to 50% power (MEDIUM). Microwave 5 minutes. Remove wax paper. Pour cranberry glaze over ham. Microwave on 50% power (MEDIUM) 2 to 3 minutes or until ham is heated through. Makes 4 servings.

Carbohydrate 9.2 g	
Protein 21.4 g	
Fat 7.5 g	

Sweet & Sour Pork

A favorite dish with half the calories of the original recipe.

1 (15-1/4-oz.) can chunk pineapple,
    packed in unsweetened pineapple juice
2 tablespoons cornstarch
3 tablespoons packed brown sugar
1/4 cup cider vinegar
2 tablespoons lite soy sauce
3/4 pound lean boneless pork (shoulder
    or leg), trimmed of excess fat,
    cut in 1/2-inch cubes

2 medium carrots, cut in thin
    diagonal slices
1/2 cup coarsely chopped onion
1/2 medium green bell pepper, seeded,
    cut in thin strips
2 cups hot, cooked rice

Drain pineapple juice in a 1-1/2-quart microwave-safe casserole dish; set pineapple chunks aside. Dissolve cornstarch in pineapple juice. Stir in brown sugar, vinegar, soy sauce and pork. Cover tightly. Microwave on 100% power (HIGH) 4 minutes. Stir; recover. Adjust power level to 30% power (MEDIUM-LOW). Microwave 12 to 14 minutes or until pork is no longer pink in center (cut to test). Set aside. In a medium microwave-safe bowl, combine carrots, onion and bell pepper. Cover tightly. Microwave on 100% power (HIGH) 3 to 4 minutes. Stir carrot mixture and reserved pineapple chunks into pork mixture. Adjust power level to 70% power (MEDIUM-HIGH). Microwave 2 to 3 minutes. Serve over rice. Makes 4 servings.

Carbohydrate 50.0 g	
Protein 18.1 g	
Fat 8.6 g	

Tip

In addition to providing plenty of protein, red meats are rich in iron—a crucial component of red blood cells. Adult women need to consume 18 milligrams of iron daily; adult men need 10 milligrams per day.

Sweet & Sour Pork, over Microwave "Steamed" Rice, page 102

Macaroni & Cheese with Turkey Ham *310 Calories*

This calcium-rich dish is ideal for those who don't drink milk.

1 cup uncooked elbow macaroni
1 cup water
1 medium green bell pepper, seeded,
  chopped
1-1/2 cups skim milk
1 tablespoon cornstarch

1/2 teaspoon dry mustard
4 ounces low-fat Cheddar
  cheese, finely diced (1 cup)
3 ounces turkey ham, chopped
Paprika to taste

In a 2-quart microwave-safe casserole dish, combine macaroni and water. Cover tightly. Microwave on 100% power (HIGH) 4 to 5 minutes or until boiling. Let stand 5 minutes. Drain; recover. Place bell pepper in a small microwave-safe bowl. Cover tightly. Microwave on 100% power (HIGH) 1 to 2 minutes. In a 4-cup glass measure, combine milk, cornstarch and mustard. Microwave on 100% power (HIGH) 3 to 4 minutes or until thickened, stirring every minute during cooking. Stir in cheese until melted. Stir bell pepper, cheese sauce and ham into macaroni. Cover tightly. Microwave on 100% power (HIGH) 4 minutes. Sprinkle with paprika. Makes 4 servings.

Carbohydrate 32.1 g	
Protein 21 g	
Fat 11.2 g	

Savory Lamb Steaks *334 Calories*

Lean and tasty lamb is a good choice for light eating—most of the fat is on the outside and can be cut away.

4 (4 oz.) lamb leg steaks,
  trimmed of excess fat
1 medium onion, coarsley chopped
1 (8-oz.) can unsalted tomato sauce
2 tablespoons dry white wine
2 tablespoons chopped fresh parsley

1 teaspoon dried leaf marjoram
1 teaspoon dried leaf rosemary
1 tablespoon cornstarch
1 tablespoon water
2 cups hot cooked noodles

Arrange steaks in a 11'' x 7'' microwave-safe dish with thickest portion toward outside of dish. Combine onion, tomato sauce, wine, parsley, marjoram and rosemary. Pour over chops. Cover tightly. Microwave on 100% power (HIGH) 5 minutes. Adjust power level to 30% power (MEDIUM-LOW). Microwave 10 minutes. Rearrange, moving outside pieces to center of dish. Recover; microwave on 30% power (MEDIUM-LOW) 20 to 25 more minutes or until done (cut to test). Remove steaks to a platter. Dissolve cornstarch in water; stir into sauce. Microwave on 100% power (HIGH) 3 to 4 minutes or until bubbly and thick. Serve steaks with sauce. Makes 4 servings.

Carbohydrate 25.9 g	
Protein 34.0 g	
Fat 8.9 g	

Vegetables

Of all the nutrients in our diet, carbohydrates are probably the least well understood by many people. It's a common belief that all carbohydrate-rich foods are fattening and should be avoided. But in fact, this is only true of *simple carbohydrates*—sugars that provide plenty of calories and very few nutrients. *Complex carbohydrates*, on the other hand—including vegetables, fruits, legumes, grains and nuts—are energizers containing fiber, essential vitamins and minerals. Carbohydrates provide the best fuel for most of the body's functions. The human brain depends on them exclusively for energy.

According to the U.S. dietary goals, 48% of our daily calories should come from complex carbohydrates. Because these nutrients play such a large part in a healthful diet, this chapter is one of the longest in our book, offering dozens of delicious, nutritious recipes. Start by choosing Teddy's Taters for breakfast or Italian Stuffed Peppers for supper; top off lunch or dinner with Zucchini Boats or Herb Stuffed Tomatoes. Good nutrition is a choice—a choice you make each time you serve up vegetables and fruits.

To assure evenly cooked vegetables, make sure they are cut in uniform shapes. A good guide to microwaving vegetables is to allow 6 minutes per pound.

Asparagus with Lemon Sauce

74 Calories

Light lemon sauce tops a favorite springtime vegetable.

1 pound fresh asparagus, washed
3 tablespoons water
1 tablespoon margarine
1 tablespoon all-purpose flour
1/2 cup skim milk

1/2 teaspoon ground ginger
1 teaspoon grated lemon peel
2 teaspoons lemon juice
Lemon slices

Snap off and discard tough stalk ends of asparagus. Arrange spears, with buds toward center, in a shallow microwave-safe dish. Sprinkle with water. Cover tightly. Microwave on 100% power (HIGH) 3 minutes. Rearrange, moving outside spears to center of dish. Recover; microwave on 100% power (HIGH) 3 minutes more or until almost tender. Let stand 5 minutes. In a 1-cup glass measure, microwave margarine on 100% power (HIGH) 45 to 50 seconds or until melted. Stir in flour. Microwave on 100% power (HIGH) 1 minute or until bubbly. Stir in milk and ginger. Microwave on 100% power (HIGH) 1 minute. Stir; microwave on 100% power (HIGH) 1 to 1-1/2 minutes more or until thickened. Stir in lemon peel and juice. Drain asparagus; arrange on a microwave-safe platter. Pour lemon sauce evenly over asparagus. Microwave on 100% power (HIGH) 50 seconds or until heated through. Garnish with lemon slices. Makes 4 servings.

Carbohydrate 9.1 g	
Protein 4.2 g	
Fat 3.2 g	

Harvard Beets

91 Calories

A lighter version of a popular sweet-tart beet dish.

1 tablespoon cornstarch
1-1/2 teaspoons lemon juice
1 cup orange juice

2 teaspoons brown sugar
1 (16-oz.) can sliced beets, drained

In a medium microwave-safe bowl, combine cornstarch, lemon juice, orange juice and brown sugar. Microwave on 100% power (HIGH) 2 to 3 minutes or until bubbly and slightly thickened, stirring every minute during cooking. Stir in beets. Microwave on 100% power (HIGH) 1-1/2 minutes or until heated through. Makes 4 servings.

Carbohydrate 21.8 g	
Protein 1.6 g	
Fat 0.3 g	

Lemon-Sesame Asparagus

60 Calories

A great complement for any main dish.

2 teaspoons sesame seeds
1 pound fresh asparagus, washed
3 tablespoons water

2 teaspoons margarine
2 teaspoons lemon juice

In a 3-ounce custard cup, microwave sesame seeds on 100% power (HIGH) 3 minutes or until golden brown. Set aside. Snap off and discard tough stalk ends of asparagus. Arrange spears, with buds toward center, in a shallow microwave-safe dish. Sprinkle with water. Cover tightly. Microwave on 100% power (HIGH) 3 minutes. Rearrange, moving outside spears to center of dish. Recover; microwave on 100% power (HIGH) 3 minutes more or until tender. Let stand 5 minutes. In a 1-cup glass measure, combine margarine and lemon juice. Microwave on 100% power (HIGH) 45 seconds. Drain asparagus. Pour sauce over asparagus. Sprinkle with toasted sesame seeds. Makes 4 servings.

Carbohydrate 4.9 g	
Protein 3.2 g	
Fat 3.7 g	

Broccoli with Herb Sauce

90 Calories

Broccoli supplies vitamins and minerals to the daily diet.

1 pound fresh broccoli, washed, cut in
   spears with 2-inch-long stems
2 teaspoons water
2 tablespoons margarine
1/4 teaspoon dried leaf chervil

1/4 teaspoon dried leaf oregano
1/4 teaspoon dried leaf basil
Dash white pepper
Salt to taste

Peel broccoli stems. Arrange broccoli, with stems to outside of dish, in a shallow 1-quart microwave-safe dish. Sprinkle with water. Cover tightly. Microwave on 100% power (HIGH) 3 minutes. Rearrange, moving outside spears to center of dish. Recover; microwave on 100% power (HIGH) 3 minutes more or until tender-crisp. Let stand 5 minutes. In a 1-cup glass measure, microwave margarine on 100% power (HIGH) 45 to 50 seconds or until melted. Stir in chervil, oregano, basil, pepper and salt. Drain broccoli. Arrange on a serving dish. Pour herb sauce over broccoli. Makes 4 servings.

Carbohydrate 6.6 g	
Protein 4.0 g	
Fat 6.5 g	

Green Beans Parmesan

47 Calories

Topped with Parmesan cheese and seasoned with garlic, these green beans make a good side dish.

1/2 pound fresh green beans,
    cut in 1-1/2-inch pieces
2 tablespoons water
1 garlic clove, minced

1/2 medium onion, sliced
2 teaspoons margarine
1-1/2 tablespoons grated Parmesan
    cheese

In a 1-1/2-quart microwave-safe casserole dish, combine beans, water, garlic and onion. Cover tightly. Microwave on 100% power (HIGH) 5 minutes. Stir; recover. Microwave on 100% power (HIGH) 4 to 6 minutes more or until fork-tender. If too crisp, microwave on 100% power (HIGH) 1 to 2 minutes more. Stir in margarine until melted. Sprinkle with cheese. Let stand 5 minutes. Makes 4 servings.

Carbohydrate 4.6 g	
Protein 1.9 g	
Fat 2.6 g	

Lima Beans

95 Calories

For a complete meal, stir diced cooked meat into lima beans.

1 (10-oz) package frozen lima beans
    (1-1/2 cups)
1 cup water

1/2 teaspoon dried leaf oregano
1/2 teaspoon dried leaf basil

In a 1-1/2-quart microwave-safe casserole dish, combine beans, water, oregano and basil. Cover tightly. Microwave on 100% power (HIGH) 5 minutes. Stir; recover. Microwave on 100% power (HIGH) 5 to 6 minutes more or until beans are tender. Let stand 5 minutes; drain. Makes 3 servings.

Carbohydrate 17 g	
Protein 6.5 g	
Fat 0.3 g	

Tip

The skin on broccoli stalks tends to become tough when microwaved, so peel broccoli stalks before cooking. Peel stems of flowerets, too, unless you've cut the flowerets with very short stems.

How to Make Broccoli with Lemon Sauce

1/Broccoli spears are arranged with stalks to the outside of the dish, then sprinkled with a little water.

2/Lemon and ginger enhance the flavor of the cheese-based sauce, heated separately and poured over the tender-crisp broccoli just before serving.

Broccoli with Lemon Sauce

126 Calories

Just one spear of broccoli provides 150% of the RDA for vitamin C.

1/4 cup slivered almonds	1 (3-oz.) package Neufchâtel cheese
2 teaspoons margarine	1/4 cup skim milk
2 pounds fresh broccoli, washed, cut in spears	1 teaspoon lemon juice
2 teaspoons water	1/2 teaspoon ground ginger

In a custard cup, combine almonds and margarine. Microwave on 100% power (HIGH) 2 to 3 minutes or until almonds are light brown. Set aside. Peel stalk of each broccoli spear. Arrange, with stalks to outside of dish, in a shallow 1-1/2-quart microwave-safe casserole dish. Sprinkle with water. Cover tightly. Microwave on 100% power (HIGH) 5 minutes. Rearrange, moving outside spears to center of dish. Recover; microwave on 100% power (HIGH) 5 to 7 minutes more or until tender-crisp. Let stand 5 minutes. Adjust power level to 30% power (MEDIUM-LOW). In a 2-cup glass measure, microwave cheese 1 minute or until softened. Stir until smooth. Beat in milk, lemon juice and ginger. Adjust power level to 50% power (MEDIUM). Microwave 1 minute or until hot. Drain broccoli. Top with sauce. Sprinkle with toasted almonds. Makes 6 servings.

Carbohydrate 10.4 g	
Protein 7.7 g	
Fat 7.6 g	

Parsley Buttered Carrots

45 Calories

Carrots contain beta-carotene, thought to be a cancer-preventative.

4 medium carrots, sliced (2 cups)
1 tablespoon margarine
1 tablespoon water

1/4 cup chopped fresh parsley
1/8 teaspoon white pepper

In a 1-1/2-quart microwave-safe casserole dish, combine carrots, margarine, water and parsley. Cover tightly. Microwave on 100% power (HIGH) 3 minutes. Stir; recover. Microwave on 100% power (HIGH) 3 to 4 minutes more or until carrots are tender. Sprinkle with pepper. Makes 4 servings.

Carbohydrate 5 g	
Protein 0.3 g	
Fat 3 g	

Glazed Carrots & Apples

106 Calories

Carrots and apples make a wonderful high-fiber combination.

1 pippin apple, peeled, cored, diced
5 medium carrots, sliced (2-1/2 cups)
1 tablespoon packed brown sugar

2 teaspoons margarine
2 tablespoons water

In a 1-quart microwave-safe casserole dish, combine apple, carrots, brown sugar, margarine and water. Cover tightly. Microwave on 100% power (HIGH) 7 to 8 minutes or until carrots are tender, stirring several times during cooking. Let stand 2 minutes. Makes 4 servings.

Carbohydrate 21.5 g	
Protein 1.5 g	
Fat 2.4 g	

Parmesan Celery

42 Calories

Pimentos add color to this crunchy vegetable dish.

3 cups diagonally sliced celery
1-3/4 ounces fresh mushrooms, sliced (3/4 cup)
1/2 cup chopped fresh parsley

1/4 cup diced pimentos
1-1/2 teaspoons margarine
2 tablespoons grated Parmesan cheese

In a 2-quart microwave-safe casserole dish, combine celery, mushrooms, parsley, pimentos and margarine. Cover tightly. Microwave on 100% power (HIGH) 5 to 7 minutes or until celery is tender, stirring several times during cooking. Drain; sprinkle with cheese. Serve immediately. Makes 4 servings.

Carbohydrate 4.8 g	
Protein 2.4 g	
Fat 1.8 g	

Cheesy Cauliflower

89 Calories

A whole head of cauliflower microwaves to tenderness in minutes without water.

1 medium head cauliflower (1-1/2 lbs.)
1 tablespoon cornstarch
1 cup skim milk
1/4 teaspoon butter-flavored salt
1 teaspoon margarine

Dash white pepper
1/2 cup shredded Cheddar cheese
  (2 oz.)

Break off outer leaves of cauliflower; trim stalk close to base. Rinse well. Wrap in wax paper. Place on a microwave-safe plate with edges of paper down. Microwave on 100% power (HIGH) 6 to 7 minutes or until fork-tender. Set aside. In a 2-cup glass measure, dissolve cornstarch in milk. Stir in butter-flavored salt, margarine and pepper. Microwave on 100% power (HIGH) 2 to 3 minutes or until thickened, stirring every minute during cooking. Stir in cheese until melted. Remove wax paper from cauliflower. Pour sauce over cauliflower. Makes 6 servings.

Carbohydrate 6.1 g	
Protein 5.1 g	
Fat 5.2 g	

Corn Pudding

Corn provides 3.9 grams dietary fiber per 1/2 cup.

1 (16-oz.) can cream-style corn
2 eggs, beaten
2 tablespoons chopped green bell pepper
2 tablespoons finely chopped onion

1/2 cup skim milk
1 tablespoon sugar
1/2 cup crushed round butter crackers
Paprika to taste

Coat a round 9-inch microwave-safe dish with cooking spray. Combine corn, eggs, bell pepper, onion, milk, sugar and crackers in prepared dish. Cover tightly. Microwave on 50% power (MEDIUM) 7 minutes. Stir; sprinkle with paprika. Adjust power level to 70% power (MEDIUM-HIGH). Microwave 4 to 5 minutes or until a knife inserted near center comes out clean. Let stand 10 minutes. Makes 6 servings.

Carbohydrate 25.7 g	
Protein 5.1 g	
Fat 3 g	

Mediterranean Vegetable Medley

A wonderful eggplant and vegetable combination.

1 medium (1-lb.) eggplant, peeled,
  cut in 1/2-inch cubes
1 medium (5-oz.) zucchini, cut in
  1/4-inch-thick slices
1 medium green bell pepper, seeded,
  diced (1 cup)

1 garlic clove, minced
1 teaspoon olive oil
1/4 teaspoon dried leaf basil
4 large pitted ripe olives, sliced
2 tomatoes, cut in wedges

In a 2-1/2-quart microwave-safe dish, combine eggplant, zucchini, bell pepper, garlic, oil and basil. Cover tightly. Microwave on 100% power (HIGH) 9 to 11 minutes or until eggplant is translucent and zucchini is tender, stirring several times during cooking. Stir in olives and tomatoes. Recover; microwave on 100% power (HIGH) 1 to 2 minutes more. Makes 6 servings.

Mediterranean Vegetable Medley

Eggplant Italiano

Save calories by steaming eggplant instead of frying it.

1 medium (1-lb.) eggplant, cut in
   1/2-inch-thick slices
1 (15-oz.) can tomato sauce
1 garlic clove, minced

1/2 teaspoon dried leaf basil
1/2 cup shredded part-skim mozzarella
   cheese (2 oz.)

Arrange eggplant slices in a single layer in an 11'' x 7'' microwave-safe dish. In a small bowl, combine tomato sauce, garlic and basil. Pour over eggplant. Cover tightly. Microwave on 100% power (HIGH) 8 to 10 minutes or until eggplant is tender. Sprinkle with cheese. Let stand 5 minutes. If necessary, microwave on 100% power (HIGH) 1 minute to melt cheese. Makes 6 servings.

Carbohydrate 12.3 g	
Protein 5.5 g	
Fat 2.4 g	

"Stir-Fried" Vegetables

Crisp and colorful, with an Oriental flavor.

1 tablespoon margarine
1 cup diagonally sliced green onions
5 stalks diagonally sliced celery (2 cups)
1 medium green bell pepper, seeded,
   chopped (1 cup)
2 carrots, thinly sliced (1 cup)

5 ounces fresh snow peas, ends and
   strings removed (1 cup)
2-1/2 ounces fresh bean sprouts (1 cup)
6 ounces fresh mushrooms, sliced (2 cups)
1/4 cup lite soy sauce
1/4 teaspoon ground ginger

In a 2-quart microwave-safe casserole dish, combine margarine, green onions, celery, bell pepper and carrots. Cover tightly. Microwave on 100% power (HIGH) 3 minutes; drain. Stir in snow peas, bean sprouts and mushrooms. Recover; microwave on 100% power (HIGH) 2 minutes. Stir; recover. Microwave on 100% power (HIGH) 2 to 3 minutes more or until vegetables are tender-crisp; drain. In a 1-cup glass measure, mix soy sauce and ginger. Pour evenly over vegetables. Microwave on 100% power (HIGH) 1 minute. Makes 8 servings.

Carbohydrate 12.3 g	
Protein 4.3 g	
Fat 1.7 g	

How to Make Stuffed Onions

1/Using a sharp knife, hollow out center of each onion leaving a 1/4-inch thick shell.

2/A colorful mix of peas, carrots, mushrooms and seasonings fill these onion shells.

Stuffed Onions

93 Calories

A wonderful vegetable dish with a gourmet touch.

4 large onions, peeled
1 (10-oz.) package frozen green peas
4 ounces fresh mushrooms, sliced (1-1/2 cups)
1/4 cup shredded carrot

1/4 teaspoon dried leaf thyme
1/8 teaspoon white pepper
1/2 teaspoon low-sodium chicken-bouillon
   granules

Using a sharp knife, hollow out center of each onion, leaving a 1/4-inch-thick shell. (Reserve centers of onions for other uses.) Place onions in a square 8-inch microwave-safe dish. Set aside. In a medium bowl, mix peas, mushrooms, carrot, thyme, pepper and bouillon granules. Fill onions with pea mixture. Cover tightly. Microwave on 100% power (HIGH) 7 to 9 minutes or until onions are tender and stuffing is heated through. Makes 4 servings.

Carbohydrate 18.3 g	
Protein 5.5 g	
Fat 0.3 g	

Baked Stuffed Potatoes

Potatoes provide good nutrition and cost just pennies.

**4 (5-1/2-oz.) baking potatoes, scrubbed,
    pierced**
1/2 cup skim milk
1/3 cup chopped green onions

1/2 teaspoon butter-flavored salt
1/8 teaspoon white pepper
**1/4 cup shredded sharp Cheddar cheese
    (1 oz.)**

Place a paper towel in bottom of microwave oven. Arrange potatoes in a circle on paper towel. Microwave on 100% power (HIGH) 9 to 11 minutes or until potatoes give slightly when squeezed. Cool; cut in 1/2 lengthwise. Scoop pulp from each potato half, leaving a 1/4-inch-thick shell, into a medium bowl. Set shells aside. Mash potato pulp. Stir in milk, green onions, butter-flavored salt and pepper. Spoon potato mixture into shells. Arrange stuffed potatoes on a microwave-safe plate. Microwave on 100% power (HIGH) 2 to 3 minutes or until heated through. Sprinkle with cheese. Makes 8 servings.

Carbohydrate 17.5 g	
Protein 3.5 g	
Fat 1.3 g	

Teddy's Taters

A perfect side dish for breakfast, lunch or dinner.

**2 (5-oz.) red thin-skinned potatoes,
    scrubbed, cut in wedges**

2 teaspoons margarine
1 teaspoon dried leaf thyme

Place potatoes in a 1-1/2-quart microwave-safe casserole dish. Dot with margarine; sprinkle with thyme. Cover tightly. Microwave on 100% power (HIGH) 3 minutes. Stir; recover. Microwave on 100% power (HIGH) 3 to 5 minutes more or until potatoes are fork-tender. Makes 4 servings.

Carbohydrate 16.4 g	
Protein 2 g	
Fat 2 g	

How to Make Scalloped Potatoes

1/Preparing the onion-white sauce mixture first speeds up the final microwave cooking time.

2/The sauce is alternately layered with sliced potatoes, which allows flavors to blend better in the short cooking time.

Scalloped Potatoes

156 Calories

Potatoes are an excellent source of vitamin C and several B vitamins, including thiamin, niacin and hard-to-get B-6.

1/4 cup onion, finely chopped
1 tablespoon margarine
3 tablespoons all-purpose flour
1/2 teaspoon dry mustard
Dash white pepper

1-1/2 cups skim milk
4 (5- to 5-1/2-oz.) white thin-skinned potatoes, scrubbed, cut in 1/4-inch-thick slices
Paprika to taste

In a 4-cup glass measure, combine onion and margarine. Cover tightly. Microwave on 100% power (HIGH) 1 minute. Stir in flour, mustard and pepper; gradually stir in milk. Microwave on 100% power (HIGH) 4 to 5 minutes or until bubbly and thickened, stirring every 2 minutes. In a 1-1/2-quart microwave-safe casserole dish, layer potato slices and sauce. Cover tightly. Microwave on 100% power (HIGH) 16 to 18 minutes or until potatoes are fork-tender. Sprinkle with paprika. Makes 6 servings.

Carbohydrate 29 g	
Protein 5.5 g	
Fat 2.2 g	

Special Sweet Potatoes

158 Calories

One sweet potato has 150% of the RDA for vitamin A.

2 (4-oz.) sweet potatoes, peeled, diced
1 tablespoon water
1 (8-oz.) can crushed pineapple
   packed in unsweetened pineapple
   juice, drained

1/8 teaspoon ground ginger
1/8 teaspoon ground nutmeg
2 teaspoons margarine

In a 1-quart microwave-safe casserole dish, combine sweet potatoes, water and pineapple. Sprinkle with ginger and nutmeg. Cover tightly. Microwave on 100% power (HIGH) 4 minutes. Stir; recover. Microwave on 100% power (HIGH) 4 to 6 minutes more or until potatoes are tender. Dot with margarine. Makes 4 servings.

Carbohydrate 33.7 g	
Protein 1.6 g	
Fat 2.4 g	

Vegetable Medley

51 Calories

Broccoli contains pectin, a type of fiber known to regulate carbohydrate absorption, which helps to keep blood sugar levels stable.

4 medium carrots, diagonally sliced (2 cups)
2 cups fresh broccoli flowerets
2 medium crookneck squash or
   zucchini, sliced (2 cups)

1/2 teaspoon seasoned salt
Dash white pepper

Arrange vegetables in concentric rings on a round microwave-safe platter: carrots around outside of platter, then broccoli and squash in center. Cover tightly. Microwave on 100% power (HIGH) 5 to 7 minutes or until vegetables are tender-crisp. Sprinkle with seasoned salt and white pepper. Makes 6 servings.

Carbohydrate 9.5 g	
Protein 3.5 g	
Fat 0.4 g	

Spaghetti Squash with Tomato Sauce   203 Calories

Spaghetti squash can be substituted for spaghetti to reduce caloric intake.

1/2 cup chopped onion
1/2 cup chopped celery
1/2 cup finely chopped carrot
1/8 teaspoon garlic powder
1 teaspoon olive oil
2 (16-oz.) cans ready-cut tomatoes
1/4 cup dry red wine

1 bay leaf
2 tablespoons chopped fresh parsley
1 teaspoon low-sodium chicken-bouillon granules
1 teaspoon dried leaf marjoram
1/2 teaspoon sugar
1/8 teaspoon black pepper
1 (3-lb.) spaghetti squash, pierced

To make sauce, in a large microwave-safe bowl, combine onion, celery, carrot, garlic powder and oil. Cover tightly. Microwave on 100% power (HIGH) 2 minutes or until onion is transparent. Stir in tomatoes, wine, bay leaf, parsley, bouillon granules, marjoram, sugar and pepper. Recover; microwave on 100% power (HIGH) 8 minutes, stirring 3 times during cooking. Adjust power level to 50% power (MEDIUM). Microwave 18 to 20 minutes or until sauce is as thick as desired. Let stand covered. Prepare Squash. Remove bay leaf from sauce; discard. Reheat sauce; serve sauce over squash. Makes 6 servings.

To Make Spaghetti Squash: Place squash on a microwave-safe plate. Microwave on 100% power (HIGH) 9 minutes. Turn squash over. Microwave on 100% power (HIGH) 7 to 9 minutes more. Let stand 10 minutes. Cut squash in 1/2. Remove and discard seeds. Using a fork, rake out strands resembling spaghetti.

Carbohydrate 45.8 g	
Protein 6.4 g	
Fat 2 g	

Peppers & Onions   57 Calories

Bell peppers are high in vitamins and fiber.

2 red or green bell peppers,
  seeded, cut in strips
1 large onion, sliced
1 teaspoon olive oil

1 garlic clove, minced
1 tablespoon lite soy sauce
2 tablespoons dry white wine

In a 2-quart microwave-safe casserole dish, combine bell peppers, onion, oil, garlic, soy sauce and wine. Cover tightly. Microwave on 100% power (HIGH) 2 minutes. Stir; recover. Microwave on 100% power (HIGH) 2 to 3 minutes more or until vegetables are tender-crisp. Makes 4 servings.

Carbohydrate 8.1 g	
Protein 1.6 g	
Fat 1.3 g	

Zucchini Boats

There's no need to precook these zucchini—you cook shells and filling all at once.

2 medium zucchini, cut in 1/2 lengthwise
1/4 cup chopped green onions
1/2 cup chopped fresh tomato
1/2 cup shredded extra-sharp Cheddar cheese (2 oz.)

1/4 teaspoon dried leaf basil
1/8 teaspoon dried leaf marjoram
1/4 teaspoon black pepper

Hollow out inside of each zucchini half, leaving a 1/4-inch-thick shell. Chop zucchini pulp. In a medium bowl, mix zucchini pulp, green onions, tomato, 1/4 cup of cheese, basil, marjoram and pepper. Fill zucchini halves with mixture, mounding well. Place in a shallow microwave-safe dish. Cover tightly. Microwave on 100% power (HIGH) 5 to 6 minutes or until zucchini is tender. Sprinkle with remaining 1/4 cup cheese. Let stand 5 minutes. Makes 4 servings.

Carbohydrate 5 g	
Protein 4.7 g	
Fat 4.8 g	

Sesame Snow Peas & Mushrooms

The bright green color of snow peas enhances the eye appeal of any meal.

8 ounces fresh snow peas, ends and strings removed
3 ounces fresh mushrooms, sliced (1 cup)

1 teaspoon sesame oil
1 tablespoon lite soy sauce

In a 1-quart microwave-safe casserole dish, combine snow peas, mushrooms, oil and soy sauce. Cover tightly. Microwave on 100% power (HIGH) 3 minutes or until peas are tender-crisp. Makes 4 servings.

Carbohydrate 9.4 g	
Protein 5.1 g	
Fat 1.7 g	

Top to bottom: Zucchini Boats, Parsley Buttered Carrots, page 88, Stir-Fried Vegetables, page 92

Italian Stuffed Peppers

224 Calories

One serving has 175% of the RDA for vitamin C.

4 medium green bell peppers
1 cup cooked long-grain white rice
1/2 pound extra-lean ground beef
3 green onions, chopped
1 (6-oz.) can tomato paste

1 teaspoon fennel seeds, crushed
1/2 teaspoon dried leaf basil
1 (1-oz.) slice low-fat Cheddar
   cheese, cut in 8 strips

Cut a slice from stem end of each bell pepper. Remove seeds and membranes. If necessary, slightly trim bottoms to sit flat. Set aside. In a medium bowl, thoroughly mix rice, beef, green onions, tomato paste, fennel seeds and basil. Fill peppers with rice mixture. Place stuffed peppers on a microwave-safe rack set in a microwave-safe dish. Cover tightly. Microwave on 100% power (HIGH) 10 to 13 minutes or until meat is no longer pink and peppers are tender. Cut to test. Top each pepper with 2 cheese strips. Makes 4 servings.

Carbohydrate 25 g	
Protein 17.1 g	
Fat 6.5 g	

Great Hollandaise Sauce

37 Calories/tablespoon

The calorie-reduced mayonnaise makes this sauce taste unbelievably rich.

1/2 cup calorie-reduced mayonnaise
2 tablespoons water
1 tablespoon lemon juice

1/4 teaspoon butter flavoring
Dash white pepper

In a 1-cup glass measure, combine mayonnaise, water, lemon juice, butter flavoring and pepper. Microwave on 50% power (MEDIUM) 1 minute or until warm. Makes 2/3 cup.

Carbohydrate 0.2 g	
Protein 0.1 g	
Fat 4.1 g	

How to Make Squash Strips

1/Zucchini and crookneck squash are cut in 1/4-inch thick strips and combined with green onions and herbs.

2/Pimento strips and a fresh basil leaf are the easy, but effective, finishing touches.

Squash Strips

46 Calories

A bright, colorful dish to serve with any entree.

1 pound crookneck squash, cut in
  1/4-inch-thick strips
1 pound zucchini, cut in
  1/4-inch-thick strips
1/4 cup chopped green onions
1/2 teaspoon dried leaf basil or
  1-1/2 teaspoons fresh chopped basil

1/4 teaspoon dried leaf thyme
Dash white pepper
Pimento strips
Fresh basil sprig, if desired

Place crookneck squash and zucchini in a 1-1/2-quart microwave-safe casserole dish. Sprinkle with green onions, basil, thyme and pepper. Cover tightly. Microwave on 100% power (HIGH) 3 minutes. Stir; recover. Microwave on 100% power (HIGH) 3 to 4 minutes more or until squash is tender. Garnish with pimento strips and basil sprig, if desired. Makes 8 servings.

Carbohydrate 10.9 g	
Protein 1.6 g	
Fat 0.3 g	

Herbed Stuffed Tomatoes

124 Calories

Tomatoes offer a nutrition bonus—they're high in vitamins A and C.

4 medium tomatoes (1-1/2 lbs.)
2 teaspoons margarine
6 ounces fresh mushrooms, coarsely
  chopped (2 cups)
1/3 cup diced celery
1/4 cup diced green onions

l garlic clove, minced
1/4 teaspoon dried leaf thyme
1/4 cup fine dry bread crumbs
1/4 cup shredded sharp Cheddar cheese
  (1 oz.)

Cut a thin slice from stem end of each tomato. Scoop out pulp and seeds (reserve for other uses) being careful not to cut through flesh. Drain tomatoes, upside down, on paper towels. In a medium microwave-safe bowl, microwave margarine on 100% power (HIGH) 45 seconds or until melted. Stir in mushrooms, celery, green onions, garlic and thyme. Cover tightly. Microwave on 100% power (HIGH) 5 minutes or until celery is tender. Stir in bread crumbs. Place tomatoes in a square 8-inch microwave-safe dish. Spoon stuffing evenly into tomatoes. Cover tightly. Microwave on 100% power (HIGH) 3 to 4 minutes or until tomatoes are tender. Sprinkle each tomato with 1 tablespoon of cheese. Makes 4 servings.

Carbohydrate 13.8 g	
Protein 5.6 g	
Fat 5.6 g	

Microwave "Steamed" Rice

112 Calories

Cooked rice keeps up to a week in the refrigerator and up to a few months in the freezer.

2 cups water
1 cup long-grain white rice

1/2 teaspoon butter-flavored salt
Chopped fresh parsley

In a 2-1/2-quart microwave-safe casserole dish, combine water, rice and butter-flavored salt. Cover tightly. Microwave on 100% power (HIGH) 10 minutes. Stir; recover. Adjust power level to 70% power (MEDIUM-HIGH). Microwave 7 minutes or until rice is tender and water is absorbed. Let stand, covered, 5 minutes. Fluff with a fork. Sprinkle with parsley. Makes 6 servings.

Carbohydrate 25.6 g	
Protein 2 g	
Fat 0.3 g	

Quick Brown Rice

117 Calories

Brown rice is packed with B vitamins.

1-1/4 cups water	1/2 cup diced green bell pepper
1/2 teaspoon butter-flavored salt	1/2 cup chopped green onions
1 cup quick-cooking brown rice	

In a 2-quart microwave-safe casserole dish, combine water and butter-flavored salt. Cover tightly. Microwave on 100% power (HIGH) 4 minutes. Stir in rice, bell pepper and green onions; recover. Adjust power level to 50% power (MEDIUM). Microwave 10 to 15 minutes or until rice is tender and water is absorbed. Fluff with a fork. Makes 6 servings.

Carbohydrate 24.9 g	
Protein 2.6 g	
Fat 0.8 g	

Herbed Rice

139 Calories

Browning rice before cooking gives it a fluffier texture.

1 cup long-grain white rice	1/2 teaspoon dried leaf marjoram
1 tablespoon margarine	1/2 teaspoon dried leaf basil
1 cup diced onion	2 teaspoons chicken bouillon granules
1 teaspoon dried leaf rosemary	2 cups hot water

In a 2-quart microwave-safe casserole dish, combine rice and margarine. Microwave on 100% power (HIGH) 7 to 8 minutes or until rice is browned, stirring every 2 minutes. Stir in onion, rosemary, marjoram, and basil. Dissolve bouillon granules in water. Stir water mixture into browned rice. Cover tightly. Microwave on 100% power (HIGH) 5 minutes. Stir; recover. Adjust power level to 30% power (MEDIUM-LOW). Microwave 20 minutes or until rice is tender and water is absorbed. Fluff with a fork. Makes 6 servings.

Carbohydrate 28.3 g	
Protein 2.4 g	
Fat 2.3 g	

Salt: Shaking the Habit

Salting is a learned habit that's easy to shake. As the amount used is reduced, we become aware of the natural flavors of foods—and learn to enjoy them "as is." If you're reducing salt intake, microwave cooking can be a big help. Don't add salt *before* microwaving; this can result in tough, rubbery cooked food.

Low-sodium cooking means learning to flavor food creatively. Season with salt-free flavor enhancers such as herbs, spices and citrus juices. (There's an extra bonus in using citrus juices—the acid they contain helps tenderize meats.) It's also a good idea to limit your use of processed foods. Though some foods, such as meats, eggs, fish, poultry and milk, naturally contain sodium, most of the extra sodium we eat is added during processing or at the table. Salt is a natural preservative, and manufacturers take advantage of this.

This chapter features 18 low-salt recipes, each providing 200 milligrams of sodium or less per serving. A number of these dishes call for tomato sauce, bouillon granules and/or soy sauce, both for convenience and for great flavor. To keep the sodium content down, though, we call for these items in their low-salt (or "lite") varieties. You can make the same substitutions when you adapt other recipes for low-sodium cooking.

Italian Pasta Soup

Quick, easy and delicious!

1/2 cup chopped onion
1 (16-oz.) can tomatoes
2 cups water
2-1/2 teaspoons low-sodium chicken
    bouillon granules

1/4 cup uncooked elbow macaroni
1/4 cup chopped fresh parsley

Place onion in an 8-cup glass measure. Cover tightly. Microwave onion on 100% power (HIGH) 1 minute. Stir in tomatoes with juice, water, bouillon granules, macaroni and parsley. Recover; microwave on 100% power (HIGH) 13 to 15 minutes or until macaroni is tender, stirring several times. Makes 6 (96 mg sodium) servings.

Carbohydrate 10 g	
Protein 2.3 g	
Fat 0.4 g	

Vegetable-Barley Stew

Unlike wheat, most varieties of barley are high in lysine, one of the essential amino acids.

1 medium onion, chopped
4 carrots, sliced
2 celery stalks, sliced
6 cups water
1 cup pearl barley

1/8 teaspoon black pepper
1 teaspoon dried leaf marjoram
1 teaspoon dried leaf thyme
1/2 cup chopped parsley
1 cup frozen green peas

In a deep 5-quart microwave-safe dish, combine onion, carrots and celery. Cover tightly. Microwave on 100% power (HIGH) 6 minutes. Stir in water and barley. Recover; microwave on 100% power (HIGH) 10 to 12 minutes or until boiling. Stir in pepper, marjoram, thyme and parsley; recover. Adjust power level to 30% power (MEDIUM-LOW). Microwave 50 to 55 minutes or until barley is tender, stirring several times during cooking. Stir in peas. Let stand 2 minutes. Makes 8 (41.8 mg sodium) servings.

Carbohydrate 29.1 g	
Protein 4.1 g	
Fat 0.5 g	

Minestrone Soup

When used in moderation, bacon can add flavor without adding excess salt.

2 bacon slices, cut in 1/2 inch pieces
3/4 cup diced onion
1/4 teaspoon garlic powder
1 carrot, thinly sliced
1 celery stalk, diced
2 tablespoons water
2 teaspoons low-sodium beef bouillon
   granules

3 cups hot water
1 (8-oz.) can unsalted tomato sauce
1 teaspoon Italian herb seasoning
1 (15-oz.) can kidney beans, drained,
   rinsed
1/2 cup uncooked elbow macaroni
1/2 cup chopped zucchini
1/4 teaspoon black pepper

In a deep 2-1/2-quart microwave-safe dish, microwave bacon on 100% power (HIGH) 2 to 3 minutes or until crisp; drain. Stir in onion, garlic powder, carrot, celery and 2 tablespoons water. Cover tightly. Microwave on 100% power (HIGH) 4 to 5 minutes or until vegetables are tender. Stir bouillon granules into 3 cups hot water until dissolved. Add to vegetables. Stir in tomato sauce, herb seasoning, beans, macaroni, zucchini and pepper; recover. Microwave on 100% power (HIGH) 15 to 20 minutes or until macaroni is tender, stirring several times during cooking. Makes 8 (181 mg sodium) servings.

Carbohydrate 17.3 g	
Protein 5.9 g	
Fat 1.4 g	

Split Pea Soup

In addition to lots of fiber, split peas provide 7 of the 9 essential amino acids needed for good health.

4 cups water
1 cup dried split peas
1 medium onion, chopped
2 carrots, sliced
1 celery stalk, diced
1/4 cup chopped fresh parsley

1 garlic clove, minced
1 teaspoon fennel seeds, crushed
1/2 teaspoon dried leaf oregano
1/2 teaspoon dried leaf thyme
1/4 teaspoon black pepper

In a 4-quart microwave-safe dish, combine water, peas, onion, carrots, celery, parsley, garlic, fennel seeds, oregano, thyme and pepper. Cover tightly. Microwave on 100% power (HIGH) 15 to 18 minutes. Stir; recover. Adjust power level to 30% power (MEDIUM-LOW). Microwave 40 to 50 minutes or until peas are tender, stirring several times during cooking. Makes 6 (39.6 mg sodium) servings.

Carbohydrate 25.1 g	
Protein 8.6 g	
Fat 0.5 g	

How to Make Smoked Turkey Breast

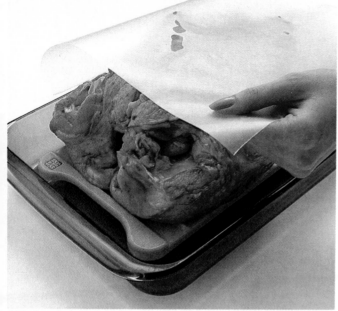

1/Turkey breast, brushed with smoke mixture, is covered with wax paper to help retain moisture and prevent spattering.

2/Remaining smoke mixture is brushed over partially-cooked turkey. Probe assures turkey cooks to proper doneness.

Smoked Turkey Breast

198 Calories

A delicious deli delight you can make without a smoker.

1 tablespoon unsalted margarine
1/2 teaspoon liquid hickory smoke
1 tablespoon browning sauce

1 teaspoon garlic powder
1/2 teaspoon ground ginger
1 whole (5-lb.) turkey breast

In a small microwave-safe bowl, microwave margarine on 100% power (HIGH) 45 to 50 seconds or until melted. Blend in liquid hickory smoke, browning sauce, garlic powder and ginger. Brush turkey breast using 1/2 of smoke mixture. Place turkey, breast down, on a microwave-safe rack set in a 13'' x 9'' microwave-safe dish. Cover with wax paper. Adjust power level to 70% power (MEDIUM-HIGH). Microwave 30 minutes. Turn turkey breast over. Brush with remaining smoke mixture. Insert probe into thickest part, not touching bone. Recover; microwave on 70% power (MEDIUM-HIGH) until probe registers 170F, about 20 minutes. Tent with foil. Let stand 15 to 20 minutes before carving. Makes 16 (75 mg sodium) servings.

Carbohydrate 0.1 g	
Protein 28 g	
Fat 8.2 g	

Dilled New Potatoes

93 Calories

Dill adds flavor to these attractive red potatoes.

4 (5- to 5-1/2-oz.) red thin-skinned potatoes, scrubbed
1/4 cup chopped green onions

1 tablespoon minced parsley
1/4 teaspoon dried dill weed
2 teaspoons unsalted margarine, melted

Peel a 1/2-inch strip around center of each potato. Arrange potatoes in a 1-quart microwave-safe dish. Sprinkle with green onions, parsley and dill weed. Cover tightly. Microwave on 100% power (HIGH) 3 minutes. Turn potatoes over. Microwave on 100% power (HIGH) 2 to 3 minutes more or until potatoes are fork-tender. Coat potatoes with margarine. Makes 4 (27 mg sodium) servings.

Carbohydrate 17 g	
Protein 2.2 g	
Fat 2 g	

Oriental Vegetables

64 Calories

Mandarin oranges add sweetness and color to this vegetable dish.

1 (22-oz.) package frozen mixed vegetables (carrots, cauliflower and broccoli)
1 tablespoon minced onion
3 ounces fresh mushrooms, sliced (1 cup)

1 (11-oz.) can mandarin orange sections
1 tablespoon unsalted margarine
1 tablespoon lite soy sauce
1 tablespoon cornstarch
2 tablespoons chopped peanuts

In a 2-quart microwave-safe dish, combine frozen vegetables, onion and mushrooms. Cover tightly. Microwave on 100% power (HIGH) 4 minutes. Stir; recover. Microwave on 100% power (HIGH) 4 to 5 minutes more or until tender-crisp. Drain; set aside. Drain mandarin orange sections; reserve 1/2 cup juice. In a 2-cup glass measure, combine reserved juice, margarine, and soy sauce. Dissolve cornstarch in juice mixture. Pour over vegetables. Microwave on 100% power (HIGH) 3 minutes, stirring every minute during cooking. Gently stir in mandarin orange sections. Sprinkle with peanuts. Makes 8 (8 mg sodium) servings.

Carbohydrate 7.8 g	
Protein 3.3 g	
Fat 2.9 g	

Smoked Turkey Breast, page 107; Asparagus with Lemon Sauce, page 84; Baked Stuffed Potatoes, page 94

Fresh Vegetable Omelet

136 Calories

A good way to use abundant summer harvest.

1/2 cup chopped onion
1-1/2 ounces fresh mushrooms, sliced (1/2 cup)
1 small crookneck squash, cut in
   1/4-inch-thick slices
1/3 cup diced green bell pepper

3 eggs
1/2 teaspoon garlic powder
1/2 teaspoon dried dill weed
1-1/2 cups shredded part-skim
   mozzarella cheese (6 oz.)

In a 9-inch microwave-safe pie plate, combine onion, mushrooms, squash and bell pepper. Cover tightly. Microwave on 100% power (HIGH) 2 minutes. Drain; set aside. In a medium bowl, beat eggs, garlic powder and dill weed. Stir in cheese; pour over vegetables. Adjust power level to 50% power (MEDIUM). Microwave 8 to 10 minutes or until center is set. Check halfway through cooking. If becoming too dry around edges, shield edges with foil. Cut in wedges to serve. Makes 6 (184 mg sodium) servings.

Carbohydrate 4.1 g	
Protein 9.6 g	
Fat 9.1 g	

Tip

Exercise is essential for staying in shape and reducing stress. If missing regular trips to the gym or other exercise workout, try parking far from stores and walking briskly back and forth from the car. Use stairs when shopping, at work and at home. Walk around the office at breaks and lunch. Move at a faster pace than usual. Do the exercises that give maximum benefits in the shortest time: aerobic dancing, rope jumping or brisk walking.

Peas & Cauliflower

One half-cup of peas contains 3.8 grams of dietary fiber.

**1 small head cauliflower, rinsed,
  broken into flowerets**
1 carrot, thinly sliced

1 (10-oz.) package frozen green peas
1/4 teaspoon white pepper

In a 1-1/2-quart microwave-safe casserole dish, combine cauliflowerets and carrot. Cover tightly. Microwave on 100% power (HIGH) 3 to 5 minutes or until vegetables are almost tender. Top evenly with peas; recover. Microwave on 100% power (HIGH) 3 to 4 minutes or until peas are hot. Stir; sprinkle with pepper. Makes 6 (56 mg sodium) servings.

Carbohydrate 9.9 g	
Protein 4 g	
Fat 0.3 g	

Lentils & Herbed Rice

To add flavor with less salt, try using low-sodium bouillon cubes—as in this recipe.

3/4 cup dried lentils
1/2 cup brown rice
1 cup chopped onion
1/2 teaspoon dried leaf basil
1/4 teaspoon dried leaf oregano
1/4 teaspoon dried leaf thyme
1/8 teaspoon garlic powder

2 low-sodium beef-bouillon cubes
2-2/3 cups water
**3/4 cup shredded farmers cheese
  (3 oz.)**
**1/4 cup shredded Cheddar cheese
  (1 oz.)**

In a 2-quart microwave-safe casserole dish, combine lentils, rice, onion, basil, oregano, thyme, garlic powder, bouillon cubes and water. Cover tightly. Microwave on 100% power (HIGH) 15 minutes or until boiling. Stir well; recover. Adjust power level to 30% power (MEDIUM-LOW). Microwave 30 to 40 minutes or until water is absorbed and lentils and rice are tender. Stir in farmers cheese; sprinkle with Cheddar cheese. Makes 6 (119 mg sodium) servings.

Carbohydrate 29.3 g	
Protein 12.3 g	
Fat 4.5 g	

Tamale Pie

Some brands of spices, such as curry and chili powders, may contain sodium; check labels before you buy.

3/4 pound extra-lean ground beef
1/2 cup chopped green bell pepper
1/2 cup chopped onion
1 garlic clove, minced
1 (8-oz.) can unsalted tomato sauce
1 teaspoon chili powder

1/4 teaspoon dried leaf basil
1/4 teaspoon black pepper
1/2 cup yellow cornmeal
1-1/2 cups water
Parsley sprig, if desired

In a microwave-safe plastic colander, combine beef, bell pepper, onion and garlic. Set colander in a microwave-safe bowl. Microwave on 100% power (HIGH) 4 to 5 minutes or until beef is no longer pink, stirring several times with a fork during cooking. In a medium microwave-safe bowl, combine beef, tomato sauce, chili powder, basil and pepper. Microwave on 100% power (HIGH) 2 minutes or until heated through. Set aside. In a 2-cup glass measure, combine cornmeal and 1/2 cup of water; set aside. In a 4-cup glass measure, microwave remaining 1 cup of water on 100% power (HIGH) 3 minutes or until boiling. Stir into cornmeal mixture. Cover tightly. Microwave on 100% power (HIGH) 1 minute. Stir; recover. Microwave on 100% power (HIGH) 1 minute more or until thickened. Spread 1/2 of cornmeal mixture in a square 8-inch microwave-safe dish. Microwave on 100% power (HIGH) 2 to 3 minutes. Spoon beef mixture over cooked cornmeal mixture. Top evenly with remaining cornmeal mixture, leaving a decorative border exposed. Microwave on 100% power (HIGH) 2 to 3 minutes or until cornmeal topping is set but not dry. Garnish with parsley sprig, if desired. Makes 6 (122 mg sodium) servings.

Carbohydrate 11.7 g	
Protein 13 g	
Fat 5.2 g	

Tip

Terrific turkey, everybody's favorite holiday bird, makes delectable eating all year round. Whether you cook a whole turkey or parts, you're assured of a healthful meal. And what's more, leftover turkey makes a perfect beginning for additional meals.

How to Make Tamale Pie

1/Spicy meat mixture is precooked separately and then spooned over cornmeal base.

2/Remaining cornmeal mixture is spread over meat, leaving a decorative border exposed.

Turkey Sausage Patties

127 Calories

Wonderful sausage flavor minus the fat.

1 pound ground turkey
1/4 cup fine dry bread crumbs
1/4 teaspoon fennel seeds, crushed
1/4 teaspoon black pepper
1/4 teaspoon ground ginger
1/4 teaspoon ground sage
1/4 teaspoon red (cayenne) pepper
Browning sauce

In a medium bowl, thoroughly mix turkey, bread crumbs, fennel seeds, black pepper, ginger, sage and red pepper. Shape in 8 (1/2-inch-thick) patties. Place patties on a microwave-safe rack set in a 13'' x 9'' microwave-safe dish. Brush both sides of patties with browning sauce. Microwave on 100% power (HIGH) 3 minutes. Rearrange, moving outside patties to center of dish. Microwave on 100% power (HIGH) 2 to 3 minutes more or until patties are firm but still moist in center (cut to test). Makes 8 (110 mg sodium) servings.

Carbohydrate 2.3 g	
Protein 17.4 g	
Fat 4.9 g	

Shrimp Quiche

An all-occasion entree.

1 (9-inch) frozen, unbaked deep-dish
  pastry shell
1 (6-oz.) package frozen cooked shrimp
1 cup shredded Swiss cheese (4 oz.)
1/2 cup chopped green onions

1 (12-oz.) can evaporated skim milk
4 eggs, beaten
1-1/2 teaspoons Dijon-style mustard
1 tablespoon all-purpose flour
Dash white pepper

Remove pastry shell from foil pan. Place in a 9-inch microwave-safe pie plate. Microwave on 70% power (MEDIUM-HIGH) 6 to 7 minutes or until underside of pastry shell is lightly spotted with brown (lift pie plate to check). Set aside. Remove shrimp from package. Place in a medium microwave-safe bowl. Adjust power level to 30% power (MEDIUM-LOW). Microwave 2 minutes; drain. Stir in cheese and green onions. Sprinkle 3/4 of mixture over bottom of microwaved pastry shell. Set aside. In a 2-cup glass measure, microwave milk on 100% power (HIGH) 3 minutes. In a medium bowl, combine eggs, mustard, flour and pepper. Gradually beat hot milk into egg mixture. Microwave on 100% power (HIGH) 1 minute. Pour over shrimp mixture in pastry shell. Sprinkle evenly with remaining shrimp mixture. Adjust power level to 50% power (MEDIUM). Microwave 7 minutes. If becoming too dry around edges, shield edges with foil. Rotate pie plate 1/2 turn. Microwave 7 to 11 minutes more or until center is set. Let stand 5 minutes before cutting. Makes 8 (166 mg sodium) servings.

Carbohydrate 15.1 g	
Protein 16.1 g	
Fat 13.1 g	

Tip

Flavor your food with herbs and spices instead of salt. For best flavor, use fresh herbs; 1 tablespoon fresh herbs is equivalent to about 1 teaspoon dried herbs.

How to Make Shrimp Quiche

1/Egg-milk mixture is gently poured over shrimp, cheese and onion in pre-baked pastry shell.

2/After microwaving, Shrimp Quiche stands 5 minutes to "set" so it can more easily be cut into wedges.

Pineapple Carrots

55 Calories

The microwave enhances the natural sugar in the carrots; pineapple adds to the sweet flavor.

**1 pound carrots, peeled,
  cut in thin strips**
**1 (8-oz.) can crushed pineapple
  packed in unsweetened pineapple
  juice**

2 teaspoons cornstarch
1 teaspoon unsalted margarine
1/4 teaspoon ground ginger

Place carrots in a 1-1/2-quart microwave-safe casserole dish. Cover tightly. Microwave on 100% power (HIGH) 4 to 5 minutes. Stir in pineapple with juice, cornstarch, margarine and ginger; recover. Microwave on 100% power (HIGH) 2 to 3 minutes or until bubbly and slightly thickened, stirring several times during cooking. Makes 6 (17.1 mg sodium) servings.

Carbohydrate 12.2 g	
Protein 0.9 g	
Fat 0.6 g	

Glazed Acorn Rings

91 Calories

Glazed acorn rings make a beautiful vegetable dish for Thanksgiving.

1 (1-lb.) acorn squash, pierced
1/2 teaspoon cornstarch
1/3 cup unsweetened apple juice

2 tablespoons raisins
1/4 teaspoon ground cinnamon
Dash ground nutmeg

Place squash on a microwave-safe plate. Microwave on 100% power (HIGH) 4 minutes. Turn over. Microwave on 100% power (HIGH) 4 minutes more or until soft when squeezed. Let stand 5 minutes. In a 2-cup glass measure, dissolve cornstarch in apple juice. Stir in raisins, cinnamon and nutmeg. Microwave on 100% power (HIGH) 2 to 3 minutes or until thickened, stirring every minute. Cut squash crosswise in 3/4-inch-thick rings. Using a spoon, remove and discard seeds. Arrange squash rings attractively on a serving plate. Pour sauce over squash rings. Makes 4 (65 mg sodium) servings.

Carbohydrate 22.5 g	
Protein 1.9 g	
Fat 0.4 g	

Zucchini Bread

123 Calories

Zucchini gives this delicious bread its moist texture—and adds nutritional value, too.

3/4 cup all-purpose flour
1/2 cup packed dark-brown sugar
1 teaspoon ground cinnamon
1/2 teaspoon baking soda
1/2 teaspoon baking powder
1/4 teaspoon salt

1 egg, lightly beaten
1 teaspoon vanilla extract
1/3 cup vegetable oil
1 cup shredded zucchini
2 tablespoons water

Line an 8'' x 4'' microwave-safe loaf pan with wax paper. In a medium bowl, combine flour, brown sugar, cinnamon, baking soda, baking powder and salt. Beat in egg, vanilla and oil. Stir in zucchini and water. Spread batter in prepared pan. Shield corners with foil. Place pan on an inverted microwave-safe pie plate. Microwave on 50% power (MEDIUM) 7 minutes. Remove foil; rotate pan 1/4 turn. Microwave on 50% power (MEDIUM) 1 to 2 minutes more or until top is shiny and springs back when lightly touched. Let stand 5 minutes. Remove from pan to a wire rack; cool completely. Makes 12 (about 3/4-inch) (145 mg sodium) slices.

Carbohydrate 14.8 g	
Protein 1.3 g	
Fat 6.7 g	

Corn Muffins

A great muffin to serve as a snack or with a small bowl of chili.

1/2 cup yellow cornmeal
1/2 cup all-purpose flour
1 teaspoon baking powder
1/2 teaspoon baking soda

1 tablespoon sugar
1/2 cup buttermilk
1 egg, lightly beaten
2 tablespoons vegetable oil

Place a paper baking cup in cups of a microwave muffin ring or custard cups. In a medium bowl, combine cornmeal, flour, baking powder, baking soda and sugar. Mix in buttermilk, egg and oil. Fill cups half full. Microwave on 100% power (HIGH) as follows or until tops spring back when lightly touched.

1 muffin: 45 seconds
2 muffins: 1 minute
3 muffins: 1 minute 15 seconds

4 muffins: 2 minutes
5 muffins: 2 minutes 15 seconds
6 muffins: 2 minutes 30 seconds

Rotate muffin ring or custard cups halfway through cooking. Remove from muffin ring or custard cups to a wire rack; cool. Makes 9 (76 mg sodium) muffins.

Carbohydrate 11.8 g		
Protein 2.4 g		
Fat 4.2 g		

Tomatoes & Zucchini

Tomatoes and crisp zucchini slices contrast in texture and color; a sprinkling of cheese adds calcium.

2 medium zucchini, cut in
   3/8-inch-thick slices
1 small onion, sliced
2 medium tomatoes, sliced

1/2 cup chopped green bell pepper
1 teaspoon dried leaf tarragon
1/2 cup shredded farmers cheese
   (2 oz.)

Spread 1/2 of zucchini slices in bottom of a 2-quart microwave-safe casserole dish. Top with 1/2 of onion slices and 1/2 of tomatoes. Repeat layers. Top with bell pepper. Sprinkle with tarragon. Cover tightly. Microwave on 100% power (HIGH) 5 to 6 minutes or until zucchini is tender-crisp. Drain; sprinkle with cheese. Recover; let stand 5 minutes or until cheese is melted. Makes 8 (45.1 mg sodium) servings.

Carbohydrate 6.3 g		
Protein 3.4 g		
Fat 1.3 g		

Desserts with Half the Sugar

Sugar is America's number one food additive. Sugar, in the form of honey, corn syrup, molasses, sucrose, lactose and other forms, goes into millions of foods. At 16 calories per teaspoon, sugar has no redeeming nutritional value other than energy and sometimes spoils our appetites for foods that contain needed nutrients. The average American consumes 500 calories of sugar each day, 115 *pounds* of sugar each year, according to USDA research.

In time, you can decrease your fondness for sugary foods. Try satisfying your sweet tooth with gifts from nature—fresh fruits. Enjoy them uncooked, or serve up traditional treats such as Banana Cream Pie, Easy Peach Cobbler and Strawberry Glacé Pie. This chapter features these three fruit favorites and more, all reduced in sugar. In some cases, naturally sweet fruit juices provide the sweetening power with great results. Using these low-sugar recipes, you can even indulge in classic desserts like cheesecake and mousse. Less than half the sugar of the traditional recipes goes into Creamy Cheesecake and Chocolate Mousse, but just one bite proves you're not missing even a bit of rich taste. Let this chapter convince you that low-sugar desserts are delicious—and best of all, you can enjoy them guilt-free!

Carrot Cake

Old-fashioned carrot cake taste at far fewer calories!

3/4 cup all-purpose flour
1 teaspoon ground cinnamon
1/2 teaspoon baking soda
1/2 teaspoon baking powder
1/2 cup packed dark-brown sugar
1/4 teaspoon salt

2 eggs, lightly beaten
1 teaspoon vanilla extract
1/3 cup vegetable oil
1 cup finely shredded carrots
Cream Cheese Frosting, below
2 tablespoons finely chopped walnuts

Coat a 9-inch microwave-safe ring pan with cooking spray. In a medium bowl, sift flour, cinnamon, baking soda, baking powder and salt. Stir in brown sugar. Beat in eggs, vanilla and oil. Stir in carrots. Spread batter evenly in prepared pan. Place pan on an inverted microwave-safe pie plate. Microwave on 50% power (MEDIUM) 3 minutes. Rotate pan 1/4 turn. Microwave on 50% power MEDIUM) 3 to 5 minutes more or until top is still slightly shiny and springs back when lightly touched. Let stand 5 minutes. Remove from pan. Cool 20 minutes on a wire rack. Invert on a serving plate. Drizzle with Cream Cheese Frosting. Sprinkle with walnuts. Makes 8 servings.

Carbohydrate 26.1 g	
Protein 2.8 g	
Fat 11.9 g	

Cream Cheese Frosting

Triple the flavor and half the fat.

1 ounce Neufchâtel cheese
3 tablespoons powdered sugar

1/4 teaspoon vanilla extract

In a 2-cup glass measure, microwave cheese on 100% power (HIGH) 15 to 20 seconds or until softened. Beat in powdered sugar and vanilla until smooth. Makes 3 tablespoons.

Carbohydrate 2.3 g	
Protein 0.3 g	
Fat 0.7 g	

Banana Bars

Temptation at its tastiest.

3/4 cup whole-wheat flour
1/2 cup all-purpose flour
1 teaspoon baking powder
1/4 teaspoon salt
1 teaspoon apple pie spice or
    pumpkin pie spice
1/3 cup packed dark-brown sugar

1 egg, lightly beaten
1/4 cup vegetable oil
1/4 cup skim milk
1 teaspoon vanilla extract
1 medium banana, mashed (1/2 cup)
Cream Cheese Frosting, page 119
2 tablespoons finely chopped walnuts

Coat a square 8-inch microwave-safe dish with cooking spray. In a large bowl, thoroughly mix flours, baking powder, salt, apple pie spice or pumpkin pie spice, brown sugar, egg, oil, milk, vanilla and banana. Spread batter in prepared dish. Shield corners with foil. Place dish on an inverted microwave-safe pie plate. Microwave on 50% power (MEDIUM) 4 minutes. Remove foil. Rotate dish 1/4 turn. Microwave on 50% power (MEDIUM) 3 to 5 minutes more or until top is still slightly shiny and springs back when lightly touched. Cool on a wire rack. Frost with Cream Cheese Frosting. Sprinkle with walnuts. Cut in bars. Makes 24 (about 2'' x 1-1/3'') bars.

Carbohydrate 8.3 g	
Protein 1 g	
Fat 2.4 g	

Tip

Shielding is a technique used to prevent overcooking. As microwave energy cannot penetrate foil, foil shields effectively slow down cooking at the corners of foods microwaved in square containers (corners cook faster than the rest of the food). You can also use foil shields to protect areas which attract too much energy—wing tips of poultry, for example.

    *Apply foil shields to food either at the start of microwaving or about halfway through. **Always be sure the foil does not touch the walls of the oven** or it will cause arcing and can ruin your microwave oven.*

How to Make Banana Bars

1/Edges of Banana Bars are protected from overcooking with a shield of aluminum foil. Place a triangular strip of foil across each corner, covering about 1 inch of batter.

2/Cooled bars are topped with Cream Cheese Frosting and sprinkled with chopped walnuts.

Chocolate Chip Squares

108 Calories

These bars taste so rich you'd never believe they're reduced in calories.

1/3 cup margarine, room temperature
1/2 cup packed brown sugar
1 egg
1/2 teaspoon vanilla extract

3/4 cup all-purpose flour
1/4 teaspoon baking powder
1/4 teaspoon salt
1/2 cup semisweet chocolate pieces

Coat a square 8-inch microwave-safe dish with cooking spray. In a medium bowl, cream margarine and brown sugar. Beat in egg and vanilla. Stir in flour, baking powder and salt. Stir in 1/4 cup of chocolate pieces. Spread batter in prepared dish. Sprinkle with remaining chocolate pieces. Shield corners with foil. Place dish on an inverted microwave-safe pie plate. Microwave on 50% power (MEDIUM) 3 minutes. Remove foil. Rotate dish 1/4 turn. Microwave on 50% power (MEDIUM) 2 to 3 minutes more or until top springs back when lightly touched. Cool 5 minutes on a wire rack. Cut in squares. Makes 16 (2'' x 2'') squares.

Carbohydrate 14.7 g	
Protein 1.3 g	
Fat 5.5 g	

Brownie Ring

Life just wouldn't be the same without brownies. Enjoy!

1/4 cup margarine, room temperature
1/3 cup sugar
2 eggs
3 tablespoons sifted unsweetened
  cocoa powder

1/2 cup all-purpose flour
1 teaspoon vanilla extract
1/4 cup chopped walnuts
1-1/2 teaspoons powdered sugar

Coat a 9-inch microwave-safe ring pan with cooking spray. In a medium bowl, cream margarine and sugar. Beat in eggs. Stir in cocoa powder, flour and vanilla. Spread batter evenly in prepared pan. Sprinkle with walnuts. Microwave on 70% power (MEDIUM-HIGH) 1-1/2 minutes. Rotate pan 1/4 turn. Microwave on 70% power (MEDIUM-HIGH) 1 to 1-1/2 minutes or until still slightly shiny on top and set but not dry. *Do not overcook; brownies should be moist.* Cool 5 minutes on a wire rack. Remove from pan. Sprinkle with powdered sugar. Cut in 12 slices. Makes 12 brownies.

Carbohydrate 10.7 g	
Protein 2.1 g	
Fat 2.8 g	

Chocolate Cupcakes

You'll think these taste too good to be low in calories.

1/2 cup sugar
3 tablespoons vegetable oil
1 egg
1 teaspoon vanilla extract
1 cup all-purpose flour
2 tablespoons sifted unsweetened
  cocoa powder

1/4 teaspoon baking soda
1/4 teaspoon baking powder
1/4 teaspoon salt
1/2 cup water
1-1/2 teaspoons sifted powdered sugar

Place a paper baking cup in 6 cups of a microwave muffin ring or glass custard cups. In a 4-cup glass measure, combine sugar, oil, egg and vanilla. Thoroughly blend in flour, cocoa, baking soda, baking powder, cinnamon, salt and water. Fill cups half full. Microwave cupcakes on 100% power (HIGH) 2 minutes. Rotate pan 1/2 turn. Microwave on 100% power (HIGH) 1 to 1-1/2 minutes more or until tops are still slightly shiny and spring back when lightly touched. Remove from ring or custard cups to a wire rack. Repeat procedure with remaining batter. Dust lightly with powdered sugar. Makes 12 cupcakes.

Carbohydrate 16.6 g	
Protein 1.7 g	
Fat 4.4 g	

Chocolate-Orange Cake

244 Calories

Orange extract adds citrus flavor to a chocolate cake.

1-1/2 cups sifted cake flour
3/4 cup sugar
1/2 cup sifted unsweetened cocoa powder
1 teaspoon baking soda
1/4 teaspoon baking powder
1 cup skim milk

1/3 cup vegetable oil
1 teaspoon orange extract
1 egg, lightly beaten
1 cup frozen whipped topping
1 orange, cut in small pieces

Coat a 2-quart microwave-safe ring pan with cooking spray. In a large bowl, sift flour, sugar, cocoa, baking soda and baking powder. Beat in milk, oil, orange extract and egg. Pour into prepared pan. Place pan on an inverted microwave-safe pie plate. Microwave on 70% power (MEDIUM-HIGH) 4 minutes. Rotate pan 1/4 turn. Microwave on 100% power (HIGH) 2 to 3 minutes more or until top is still slightly shiny and springs back when lightly touched. Cool 5 minutes. Invert on a wire rack; cool completely. To serve, top with whipped topping and orange pieces. Makes 10 servings.

Carbohydrate 34.2 g	
Protein 4.6 g	
Fat 9.8 g	

Pineapple Bread Pudding

112 Calories

Enjoy this satisfying old-fashioned dessert in just minutes.

3 slices day-old whole-wheat bread, cubed
1/4 cup raisins
1 (8-oz.) can crushed pineapple packed
  in unsweetened pineapple juice, drained
1/2 cup skim milk

2 eggs
1 teaspoon vanilla extract
1/2 teaspoon ground cinnamon
2 tablespoons packed light-brown sugar

In a 1-1/2-quart microwave-safe dish, combine bread, raisins and pineapple. In a small bowl, beat milk, eggs and vanilla. Pour over bread mixture. In a glass custard cup, mix cinnamon and brown sugar. Sprinkle over bread mixture. Microwave on 50% power (MEDIUM) 11 to 13 minutes or until a knife inserted just off-center comes out clean. Makes 6 servings.

Carbohydrate 20.3 g	
Protein 4 g	
Fat 2.3 g	

Creamy Cheesecake Pie

Choose Neufchâtel over cream cheese—it has just 73 calories per ounce versus 100 calories per ounce for cream cheese.

1 (8-oz.) package Neufchâtel cheese	3/4 cup plain low-fat yogurt
1/4 cup sugar	2 teaspoons sugar
1 egg, lightly beaten	1/2 teaspoon almond extract
1/2 teaspoon vanilla extract	2 kiwifruit, peeled, sliced
1 Graham Cracker Crumb Crust, cooled, page 128	1 cup sliced fresh strawberries
	Fresh mint sprig, if desired

In a medium microwave-safe bowl, microwave cheese on 30% power (MEDIUM-LOW) 1-1/2 minutes or until softened. Beat in sugar, egg and vanilla until smooth. Pour into crust. Adjust power level to 50% power (MEDIUM). Microwave 4 to 5-1/2 minutes or until a knife inserted just off-center comes out clean. In a small bowl, combine yogurt, 2 teaspoons sugar and almond extract. Spoon over cheesecake. Carefully spread to edges. Microwave on 50% power (MEDIUM) 2 to 3 minutes. Cool on a wire rack. Refrigerate until cold to set center. To serve, arrange kiwifruit and strawberries in concentric circles. Garnish with mint sprig, if desired. Makes 8 servings.

Carbohydrate 25.5 g	
Protein 6.2 g	
Fat 11.6 g	

Tip

A catch phrase in the world of nutrition is "nutrient density," a rating arrived at by comparing a food's calories to the nutrients it provides. The fewer the calories and the greater the amount of nutrients, the higher the nutrient density. "Calorie-dense" foods, on the other hand, are high in calories and low in nutrients. A potato is nutrient-dense; candy is calorie-dense. Beware of calorie-dense foods—they offer few health benefits.

How to Make Creamy Cheesecake Pie

/Creamy filling is poured into quickly-prepared graham cracker crust.

2/Decorate pie with concentric circles of sliced strawberries and kiwifruit shortly before serving.

Fruit & Pudding

143 Calories

French vanilla pudding conceals a layer of fresh berries. Use blueberries or other seasonal fruit in place of strawberries, if desired. Photo on cover.

1 (4-oz.) package French vanilla pudding mix
2 cups skim milk

1 pint fresh strawberries
4 fresh mint sprigs

In a 4-cup glass measure, dissolve pudding mix in 1/2 cup of milk. Stir in remaining milk. Microwave on 100% power (HIGH) 4 minutes. Stir; microwave on 100% power (HIGH) 1 to 2 minutes more or until pudding comes to a full boil and begins to thicken. Cool; refrigerate to completely chill. Assemble just before serving. Select 4 berries for garnish. Slice; set aside. Slice remaining berries. Place 1/4 of sliced berries in each dessert dish. Spoon pudding over berries. Arrange reserved sliced berries over top of puddings. Garnish with mint sprigs. Makes 4 servings.

Carbohydrate 25.7 g	
Protein 4.7 g	
Fat 1.6 g	

Strawberry Glacé Pie

148 Calories

Strawberries offer more than great flavor; they're high in fiber and low in calories.

1 (9-inch) frozen, unbaked,
   deep-dish pastry shell
4 cups fresh whole strawberries, hulled
1/3 cup sugar

1-1/2 tablespoons cornstarch
1/4 cup water
1 teaspoon lemon juice

Transfer pastry shell from foil pan to a 9-inch microwave-safe pie plate. Prick with a fork. Microwave on 70% power (MEDIUM-HIGH) 4 minutes or until underside of pastry shell is lightly spotted with brown (lift pie plate to check). Arrange 2-1/2 cups of berries, hulled-side down, in pastry shell. Refrigerate. In a food processor fitted with a metal knife or in a blender, process remaining berries to a puree. In a 4-cup glass measure, dissolve sugar and cornstarch in water. Stir in berry puree. Microwave on 100% power (HIGH) 4 to 5 minutes or until clear and thickened, stirring every minute during cooking. Stir in lemon juice. Cool slightly. Pour over berries in pastry shell. Refrigerate until glaze is set. Makes 8 servings.

Carbohydrate 22.8 g	
Protein 1.5 g	
Fat 6.1 g	

Lemon Rice Pudding

181 Calories

A nutritious rice pudding flavored with real lemon. Photo on page 127.

1 cup cooked rice
1/4 cup sugar
2 eggs, slightly beaten
1-1/2 teaspoons lemon extract
2 teaspoons grated lemon peel

1-1/2 cups skim milk
Ground nutmeg
Lemon slices, if desired
Fresh mint leaves, if desired

In a 2-quart microwave-safe dish, combine rice and sugar. Spread in an even layer; set aside. In a small bowl, beat eggs, lemon extract and lemon peel. Set aside. In a 2-cup glass measure, microwave milk on 100% power (HIGH) 1-1/2 minutes or until warm. Gradually add milk to egg mixture, stirring constantly. Pour milk-egg mixture over rice mixture in dish. Adjust power level to 30% power (MEDIUM-LOW). Microwave 18 to 21 minutes or until a knife inserted in center comes out clean, rotating dish 1/4 turn several times during cooking. Spoon into 4 dessert glasses; dust with nutmeg. Serve warm or cold. Garnish with lemon slices and mint leaves, if desired. Makes 4 servings.

Carbohydrate 29.6 g	
Protein 7.6 g	
Fat 3.2 g	

Clockwise from upper left: Lemon Rice Pudding; Chocolate Mousse, page 130; Strawberry Glacé Pie

Graham Cracker Crumb Crust

78 Calories/1/8 of crust

Save calories by using this crumb crust in place of the traditional pastry crust.

2 tablespoons margarine
3/4 cup graham cracker crumbs

1 tablespoon sugar

In a 9-inch microwave-safe pie plate, microwave margarine on 100% power (HIGH) 55 to 60 seconds or until melted. Using a fork, combine margarine, cracker crumbs and sugar. Press mixture evenly over bottom and up sides of pie plate. Microwave on 100% power (HIGH) 1 minute or until set. Cool on a wire rack.

Carbohydrate 11.9 g	
Protein 1.1 g	
Fat 3.2 g	

Crustless Blueberry Pie

115 Calories

No crust is needed for this yummy high-fiber treat.

3 cups fresh or frozen unsweetened
  blueberries
1/3 cup sugar
3 tablespoons all-purpose flour
1/2 teaspoon grated lemon peel

1 teaspoon ground cinnamon
1/4 teaspoon ground nutmeg
1/2 cup quick-cooking rolled oats
2 tablespoons packed brown sugar
1-1/2 tablespoons firm margarine

If using frozen berries, in an 8-cup glass measure, microwave berries on 100% power (HIGH) 2 to 3 minutes; drain. In a large bowl, mix berries, sugar, flour, lemon peel, 1/2 teaspoon of cinnamon and nutmeg. Pour mixture into a 9-inch microwave-safe pie plate. In a small bowl, combine rolled oats, brown sugar and remaining 1/2 teaspoon cinnamon. Using a pastry blender or 2 knives, cut in margarine until mixture is crumbly. Sprinkle over berry mixture. Microwave on 100% power (HIGH) 5 minutes. Rotate dish 1/4 turn. Adjust power level to 50% power (MEDIUM). Microwave 4 to 5 minutes or until filling is bubbly and thickened. Serve warm. Makes 8 servings.

Carbohydrate 23.3 g	
Protein 1 g	
Fat 2.6 g	

Sugarless Apple Pie

220 Calories

The sweetness comes from the natural sugar of apple juice.

1 (6-oz.) can frozen concentrated
   apple juice
1-1/2 tablespoons cornstarch
1 teaspoon ground cinnamon
1/2 teaspoon ground nutmeg

5 to 6 Golden Delicious apples,
   peeled, cored, sliced (6 cups)
1 tablespoon margarine, chopped
1 Graham Cracker Crumb Crust,
   opposite

In an 8-cup glass measure, microwave apple juice on 100% power (HIGH) 1 minute or until thawed. Stir in cornstarch, cinnamon and nutmeg. Stir in apples and margarine. Cover with wax paper. Microwave on 100% power (HIGH) 4 minutes. Stir; microwave on 100% power (HIGH) 5 minutes or until apples are fork-tender. Cool 20 to 30 minutes. Spoon into crumb crust. Cool completely before serving. Makes 8 servings.

Carbohydrate 38.3 g	
Protein 1.4 g	
Fat 7.9 g	

Banana Cream Pie

219 Calories

Enjoy this low-fat dessert—without going off your diet.

3 tablespoons cornstarch
1/2 teaspoon salt
1/4 cup sugar
2 cups skim milk
2 egg yolks
1 teaspoon vanilla extract

1 tablespoon margarine, melted
Few drops yellow food coloring, if desired
2 medium bananas, cut crosswise in 1/2-inch slices
1 Graham Cracker Crumb Crust,
   opposite
1/2 cup frozen whipped topping, thawed

In 4-cup glass measure, mix cornstarch, salt and sugar. Gradually whisk in milk, egg yolks, vanilla, margarine and food coloring, if desired. Microwave on 100% power (HIGH) 5 to 6 minutes or until thickened, stirring every minute during cooking. Cool. Arrange bananas over bottom of crumb crust. Pour cooled cream over bananas. Refrigerate until cold. Garnish with whipped topping. Makes 8 servings.

Carbohydrate 29.7 g	
Protein 4.2 g	
Fat 9.2 g	

Chocolate Mousse

Liz Taylor's favorite dessert. Photo on page 127.

1 (1/4-oz.) envelope unflavored gelatin
  (about 1 tablespoon)
2 cups skim milk
1 egg
1/2 cup milk chocolate pieces
1/4 cup sugar

1 tablespoon cornstarch
1 teaspoon vanilla extract
1/4 cup instant nonfat dry milk powder
1/4 cup ice water
8 raspberries, if desired
Fresh mint leaves, if desired

In an 8-cup glass measure, sprinkle gelatin over 1-1/2 cups of skim milk. Let stand 5 minutes or until softened. Microwave on 100% power (HIGH) 2 minutes or until gelatin is dissolved, stirring every minute during cooking. Set aside. Separate egg; place egg white in a 4-cup glass measure. Cover tightly; refrigerate. In a small bowl, beat egg yolk. Gradually beat into gelatin mixture; set aside. In a small microwave-safe bowl, microwave chocolate pieces on 100% power (HIGH) 2 minutes or until melted. Add chocolate and sugar to gelatin mixture. Dissolve cornstarch in remaining 1/2 cup of skim milk. Stir into gelatin mixture until well blended. Microwave on 100% power (HIGH) 4 to 5 minutes or until mixture comes to a boil, stirring every minute during cooking. Stir in vanilla. Refrigerate mixture until slightly thickened. Refrigerate beaters of electric mixer until cold. Stir milk powder and ice water into chilled egg white. Beat with chilled beaters until stiff. Fold in thickened chocolate mixture. Pour into 8 small bowls or dessert dishes. Refrigerate until set. Just before serving, garnish with raspberries and mint leaves, if desired. Makes 8 servings.

Carbohydrate 18.4 g	
Protein 5.3 g	
Fat 4.6 g	

Tip

To add calcium to the non-milk-drinker's diet, try serving microwaved desserts made with skim milk.

How to Make Chocolate Mousse

1/Sprinkle gelatin over milk to soften. Let stand 5 minutes. Then microwave until completely dissolved.

2/Fold chocolate mixture into beaten egg white mixture by cutting through center, then lifting mixture up and over upon itself. Repeat to incorporate all whites.

Pumpkin Pudding Bake

143 Calories

This delicious snack also makes a timely Thanksgiving dessert.

2 eggs, beaten
1 cup canned solid-pack pumpkin
1/3 cup packed brown sugar
1/2 teaspoon pumpkin pie spice

1/4 teaspoon grated orange peel
1 (12-oz.) can evaporated skim milk
2 tablespoons chopped walnuts

In an 4-cup glass measure, combine eggs, pumpkin, brown sugar, pumpkin pie spice and orange peel. Stir in evaporated milk. Microwave on 100% power (HIGH) 5 to 6 minutes or until thickened, stirring every minute during cooking. Pour into 6 glass custard cups. Arrange custard cups in a circle in microwave oven. Adjust power level to 50% power (MEDIUM). Microwave 7 to 9 minutes or until a knife inserted just off-center comes out clean, rearranging every 2 minutes during cooking. Sprinkle with walnuts. Makes 6 servings.

Carbohydrate 22 g	
Protein 6.8 g	
Fat 3.7 g	

Miniature Cheesecake Cups

168 Calories

For an attractive dessert tray, try topping these cheesecake cups with a variety of different-colored fresh fruits.

1 (8-oz.) package Neufchâtel cheese
1/4 cup sugar
1 egg
1 tablespoon lemon juice

1/2 teaspoon vanilla extract
6 vanilla wafers
1/2 cup fresh whole strawberries,
**   hulled, or other fresh fruit**

In a 4-cup glass measure, microwave cheese on 30% power (MEDIUM-LOW) 1-1/2 minutes or until softened. Beat in sugar, egg, lemon juice and vanilla until smooth. Place a paper baking cup in 6 cups of a microwave muffin ring or custard cups. Place a vanilla wafer, flat-side down, in bottom of each cup. Top evenly with cheese mixture. Adjust power level to 50% power (MEDIUM). Microwave 2 minutes. Rotate ring or custard cups 1/2 turn. Microwave 2 to 2-1/2 minutes more or until set in center. Remove to a wire rack; cool. Refrigerate until cold. To serve, top with fruit. Makes 6 servings.

Carbohydrate 13.8 g	
Protein 5.1 g	
Fat 10.5 g	

Raspberry-Peach Cheesecake

241 Calories

An elegant and luscious dessert.

1 Graham Cracker Crust, cooled, page 128
1 (8-oz.) package Neufchâtel cheese
1/4 cup sugar
1/3 cup plain low-fat yogurt

1 egg, lightly beaten
1 teaspoon almond extract
1 (8-oz.) can sliced peaches, drained
1/3 cup low-sugar red raspberry spread

In a medium microwave-safe bowl, microwave cheese on 30% power (MEDIUM-LOW) 1-1/2 minutes or until softened. Beat in sugar, yogurt, egg and almond extract until smooth. Arrange peaches in a single layer over bottom of crumb crust. Top evenly with cheese mixture. Adjust power level to 70% power (MEDIUM-HIGH). Microwave 4 to 6 minutes or until a knife inserted just off-center comes out clean. Cool on a wire rack. Top with raspberry spread. Refrigerate until cold. Makes 8 servings.

Carbohydrate 29.7 g	
Protein 5.6 g	
Fat 12 g	

Cinnamon Apple Slices

62 Calories

Use these spiced apples for a garnish, a snack or a simple dessert.

2 Red or Golden Delicious apples,
  peeled, cored, sliced

1 tablespoon packed brown sugar
Ground cinnamon to taste

Arrange apples in an single layer on a microwave-safe plate. Sprinkle with brown sugar and cinnamon. Cover tightly. Microwave on 100% power (HIGH) 3 to 4 minutes or until fork-tender. Serve warm or cold. Makes 4 servings.

Carbohydrate 15.7 g	
Protein 0.2 g	
Fat 0.5 g	

Baked Orange Bananas

94 Calories

This dessert is high in potassium, needed to regulate the heart.

1/4 cup orange juice
2 tablespoons sugar
1/4 teaspoon ground cinnamon
1/4 teaspoon ground nutmeg

Dash ground cloves
1 teaspoon grated orange peel
3 large firm bananas, peeled

In a 1-cup glass measure, combine orange juice, sugar, cinnamon, nutmeg, cloves and orange peel. Stir until sugar dissolves. Microwave on 100% power (HIGH) 45 seconds. Cut bananas in 1/2 lengthwise, then in thirds crosswise. Arrange banana pieces in a 9-inch microwave-safe pie plate. Pour sauce over bananas. Microwave on 100% power (HIGH) 2 minutes. Rearrange, moving outside pieces to center of dish; baste. Microwave 1 to 2 minutes more or until bananas are slightly soft but not mushy. Serve warm. Makes 6 servings.

Carbohydrate 24.4 g	
Protein 1.3 g	
Fat 0.3 g	

Baked Pears

96 Calories

Using grape juice as a natural sweetener adds sweet-natural flavor.

2 ripe pears, halved, cored
1 teaspoon cornstarch
1/2 cup unsweetened white grape juice
1 teaspoon raisins

1/2 teaspoon ground cinnamon
Dash ground nutmeg
2 teaspoons sugar

Arrange pears, cut-side up, in an square 8-inch microwave-safe dish; set aside. In a 2-cup glass measure, dissolve cornstarch in grape juice. Stir in raisins, cinnamon, nutmeg and sugar. Microwave on 100% power (HIGH) 1-1/2 to 2 minutes or until thickened, stirring several times during cooking. Cool; pour glaze over pears. Cover tightly. Microwave on 100% power (HIGH) 3 to 4 minutes or until pears are fork-tender. Serve warm. Makes 4 servings.

Carbohydrate 24.2 g	
Protein 0.8 g	
Fat 0.4 g	

Apple Crisp

156 Calories

Sweetness with half the sugar.

5 Golden Delicious apples, peeled,
  cored, sliced (5 cups)
1 tablespoon lemon juice
3 tablespoons packed brown sugar
1/3 cup quick-cooking rolled oats

2 tablespoons all-purpose flour
1 teaspoon ground cinnamon
1/8 teaspoon ground nutmeg
3 tablespoons firm margarine

Arrange apples evenly in a square 8-inch microwave-safe dish. Sprinkle with lemon juice. In a small bowl, combine brown sugar, rolled oats, flour, cinnamon and nutmeg. Using a pastry blender or 2 knives, cut in margarine until mixture is crumbly. Sprinkle over apples. Cover tightly. Microwave on 100% power (HIGH) 5 minutes. Uncover; microwave on 100% power (HIGH) 3 to 4 minutes more or until apples are fork-tender. Serve warm. Makes 6 servings.

Carbohydrate 30 g	
Protein 0.8 g	
Fat 4.8 g	

How To Make Pineapple Fruit Flambé

1/Halve pineapple lengthwise. Remove fruit in chunks, leaving a 1/2-inch-thick shell.

2/Just before serving, warmed rum is poured over the fruit-filled shells and carefully ignited.

Pineapple Fruit Flambé

101 Calories

A flaming finale for a special occasion.

1 medium pineapple, halved lengthwise
1 (11-oz.) can mandarin orange sections,
    drained
1 cup sliced fresh strawberries

1 cup fresh melon balls
1/2 cup fresh blueberries
1/2 cup low-sugar strawberry spread
1/4 cup light rum

Remove fruit in chunks from each pineapple half, leaving a 1/2-inch-thick shell. Cut pineapple in cubes. In a large bowl, combine pineapple, orange sections, strawberries, melon balls, blueberries and strawberry spread. Fill pineapple halves with fruit mixture. Place halves on a large microwave-safe platter. Cover with wax paper. If using probe, insert probe through wax paper into center of fruit mixture. Microwave on 100% power until probe registers 120F. Or, microwave on 100% 4 to 5 minutes; set aside. In a 1-cup glass measure, microwave rum on 100% power (HIGH) 25 seconds. Pour hot rum over fruit mixture; carefully ignite. Let flames subside; serve. Makes 10 servings.

Carbohydrate 23.1 g	
Protein 1 g	
Fat 0.4 g	

Fresh Peach Pie

166 Calories

White grape juice contributes sweetening power to this pie.

1 (9-inch) frozen, unbaked,
  deep-dish pastry shell
8 fresh peaches, peeled, pitted
1/4 cup sugar

1 tablespoon cornstarch
1/4 teaspoon ground allspice
1/3 cup unsweetened white grape juice

Remove pastry shell from foil pan. Place in a 9-inch micrwave-safe pie plate. Microwave on 70% power (MEDIUM-HIGH) 6 to 7 minutes or until underside of pastry shell is lightly spotted with brown (lift pie plate to check). Set aside. In a food processor fitted with a metal blade or in a blender, process 2 peaches to a puree. Set aside. In an 8-cup glass measure, combine sugar and cornstarch. Stir in peach puree, allspice and grape juice. Microwave on 100% power (HIGH) 4 to 6 minutes or until clear and thickened, stirring every 2 minutes during cooking. Slice remaining 6 peaches. Layer sliced peaches in pastry shell. Spoon peach glaze evenly over peaches. Carefully spread to edges. Refrigerate several hours or until glaze is set. Makes 8 servings.

Carbohydrate 28.1 g	
Protein 1.6 g	
Fat 5.8 g	

Microwave "Stewed" Rhubarb

61 Calories

Rhubarb is refreshingly tart. It is available fresh in the spring and frozen year-round.

2 cups uncooked fresh rhubarb, cut in
  1-inch pieces

1/4 cup sugar

Place rhubarb in a 1-1/2-quart microwave-safe dish. Cover tightly. Microwave on 100% power (HIGH) 4 to 5 minutes or until rhubarb is very soft. Stir in sugar. Makes 4 servings (1/2 cup).

Carbohydrate 15.2 g	
Protein 0.5 g	
Fat 0.1 g	

Peppermint Pears

An attractive dessert or salad. Try it with a holiday meal.

1 (8-1/2-oz.) can pear halves,
  packed in juice, drained
6 maraschino cherries
2 cups water

1 (.35-oz.) package sugar-free
  lime-flavored gelatin
1 drop peppermint extract

Coat a 9'' x 5'' microwave-safe loaf pan with cooking spray. Remove excess spray with a paper towel, leaving only a "gloss" in pan. Arrange pears, cut-side down, and cherries in pan. Set aside. In a 4-cup glass measure, microwave 1 cup of water on 100% power (HIGH) 3 minutes or until boiling. Dissolve gelatin in boiling water. Stir in remaining 1 cup of water and peppermint extract. Pour gelatin mixture over pears and cherries. Refrigerate until firm. Cut in 4 rectangles. Makes 4 servings.

Carbohydrate 21.4 g	
Protein 1.6 g	
Fat 0.6 g	

Pumpkin Pie

A perfect calorie-reduced holiday dessert.

1 (9-inch) frozen, unbaked,
  deep-dish pastry shell
2 eggs, slightly beaten
1 (16-oz.) can solid-pack pumpkin
1/2 cup sugar

1/4 teaspoon salt
1 teaspoon ground cinnamon
1/2 teaspoon ground ginger
1/8 teaspoon ground allspice
1 (12-oz.) can evaporated skim milk

Remove pastry shell from foil pan. Place in a 9-inch microwave-safe pie plate. Microwave on 70% power (MEDIUM-HIGH) 6 to 7 minutes or until underside of pastry shell is lightly spotted with brown (lift pie plate to check). Set aside. In an 8-cup glass measure, combine eggs, pumpkin, sugar, salt, cinnamon, ginger and allspice. Stir in milk. Microwave on 100% power (HIGH) 6 to 8 minutes or until slightly thickened, stirring every 2 minutes during cooking. Pour into pastry shell. Adjust power level to 50% power (MEDIUM). Microwave 7 to 10 minutes or until a knife inserted just off-center comes out clean. Makes 8 servings.

Carbohydrate 30.4 g	
Protein 6.9 g	
Fat 7.5 g	

Entertaining the Light Way

Entertaining is one of life's greatest pleasures. But having a party no longer means setting up a table laden with dozens of fattening foods. Skinny foods are in fashion these days! Using your microwave oven and plenty of imagination, you can easily create a low-calorie party. Where do we start?

The most sophisticated parties begin with rich-tasting appetizers. Try Spinach Balls, succulent Stuffed Mushrooms or creamy Clam Dip. Use fresh vegetables for dippers in place of high-salt, high-fat chips and crackers. You'll also find main dishes and desserts in this chapter. All are quick and easy recipes that help make party-giving fun and hassle-free. For more entertaining ideas, look through the rest of this book. Every chapter features recipes just right for serving guests. It doesn't take long to discover that light entertaining is deliciously satisfying, a trend to make permanent in your healthy lifestyle. Bon appetit!

"Fried" Zucchini or Mushrooms

56 Calories

Serve these delicious hot appetizers with low-fat ranch-type salad dressing as a dip.

1/3 cup margarine
1/3 cup Italian-style seasoned
  bread crumbs
1/4 cup grated Parmesan cheese (3/4 oz.)

1 teaspoon dried leaf basil
1 teaspoon paprika
3 zucchini, cut in 2" x 1/2" strips
  or 32 medium, fresh mushrooms

In a 2-cup glass measure, microwave margarine on 100% power (HIGH) 1 minute or until melted. In a plastic bag, combine bread crumbs, cheese, basil and paprika. Dip zucchini or mushrooms in melted margarine. Shake in crumb mixture to coat evenly. Arrange vegetables on a microwave-safe rack set in a microwave-safe dish. Cover with a paper towel. Microwave on 100% power (HIGH) 2 minutes. Rearrange, moving outside pieces to center of dish; recover. Microwave on 100% power (HIGH) 1 to 3 minutes more or until heated through. Makes 16 servings.

Carbohydrate 3.2 g	
Protein 1.7 g	
Fat 4.2 g	

Stuffed Mushrooms

29 Calories

A special, nutritious party finger food.

8 ounces large fresh mushrooms (about 12)
3 green onions, chopped

1 tablespoon dairy sour cream
1/2 teaspoon garlic powder

Remove mushroom stems from caps. Set caps aside; finely chop stems. Place in a medium microwave-safe bowl. Stir in green onions. Cover tightly. Microwave on 100% power (HIGH) 1 minute; drain. Stir in sour cream and garlic powder. Spoon filling into mushroom caps. Arrange mushrooms in a circle, filled-side up, on a microwave-safe plate. Adjust power level to 70% power (MEDIUM-HIGH). Microwave 2-1/2 to 3-1/2 minutes. Serve warm. Makes 4 servings.

Carbohydrate 4 g	
Protein 1.8 g	
Fat 0.9 g	

Tip

Make your own Italian-style bread crumbs by mixing fine dry bread crumbs with Italian herb seasoning or a mixture of your favorite herbs.

Spinach Balls

43 Calories/appetizer

A quick party appetizer you can prepare ahead and freeze.

1 (10-oz.) package frozen spinach
1 cup bread-stuffing mix
1/2 cup finely chopped onion

2 eggs, lightly beaten
1/3 cup grated Parmesan cheese
   (1 oz.)

Remove wrapper from spinach package. Place unopened package in a microwave-safe bowl. Microwave on 100% power (HIGH) 4 to 5 minutes. Drain spinach; press out all water. In a medium bowl, combine spinach, bread-stuffing mix, onion, eggs and cheese. Shape mixture into 20 (1-inch) balls. Arrange balls in a circle on a microwave-safe plate. Adjust power level to 70% power (MEDIUM-HIGH). Microwave 2 minutes. Rearrange, moving outside balls to center of dish. Microwave on 100% power (HIGH) 1 to 3 minutes more or until firm throughout but still moist. Makes 20 appetizers.

Carbohydrate 3 g	
Protein 1.9 g	
Fat 2.7 g	

Nachos

128 Calories

The cheesy snack of the great Southwest.

24 round tortilla chips
1/2 cup shredded sharp Cheddar cheese
   (2 oz.)

2 tablespoons canned diced green
   chilies, drained

Arrange 12 tortilla chips in a circle on a large microwave-safe plate. Place 1 teaspoon cheese on top of each chip. Top cheese with 1/4 teaspoon chilies. Microwave on 70% power (MEDIUM-HIGH) 1 minute or until cheese is melted. Repeat procedure with remaining chips. Makes 4 servings.

Carbohydrate 10.3 g	
Protein 5 g	
Fat 7.7 g	

Marinated Veggies

43 Calories

Use this marinade with a variety of fresh vegetables; try it with mushrooms, zucchini or blanched green beans. Photo on page 143.

1 (15-oz.) can unsalted tomato sauce
1/2 cup water
3/4 cup thinly sliced celery
1 teaspoon garlic powder
1/4 teaspoon dried dill weed
1/2 teaspoon dried leaf oregano

1/4 teaspoon dried leaf tarragon
3/4 cup fresh cauliflowerets
1 cup fresh broccoli flowerets
1 cup diagonally sliced carrots,
   1/4-inch thick

In a 2-quart microwave-safe casserole dish, combine tomato sauce, water, celery, garlic powder, dill weed, oregano and tarragon. Cover tightly. Microwave on 100% power (HIGH) 6 minutes or until boiling. Stir in cauliflowerets, broccoli and carrots. Recover; adjust power level to 70% power (MEDIUM-HIGH). Microwave 4 to 6 minutes or until vegetables are tender-crisp, stirring several times during cooking Serve warm or cold. Makes 8 servings.

Carbohydrate 8.9 g	
Protein 2.2 g	
Fat 0.2 g	

Crunchy Vegetable Rounds

14 Calories/appetizer

Vegetables substitute for crackers in this easy hors d'oeuvre. Photo on page 5.

1/4 cup diced green onions
3 tablespoons chopped fresh mushrooms
3 tablespoons shredded carrot
2 teaspoons oil-free Italian salad dressing

1 medium cucumber or zucchini, cut
   in 14 (1/4-inch-thick) slices
1/4 cup shredded part-skim mozzarella
   cheese (1 oz.)

In a small microwave-safe bowl, combine green onions, mushrooms, carrot and dressing. Cover tightly. Microwave on 100% power (HIGH) 2 minutes. Top cucumber or zucchini slices evenly with green onion mixture. Sprinkle with cheese. Place vegetable rounds in a circle on a microwave-safe plate. Adjust power level to 70% power (MEDIUM-HIGH). Microwave 1 to 2 minutes or until cheese is melted. Makes 14 appetizers.

Carbohydrate 1.2 g	
Protein 0.9 g	
Fat 0.8 g	

Potato Skins

Deep-frying is not necessary for these delicious skins.

3 (5-1/2 oz.) baking potatoes,
  scrubbed, pierced
1 tablespoon margarine
1/4 teaspoon dried dill weed

Dash hot pepper sauce
3/4 cup shredded Swiss cheese
  (3 oz.)
3 green onions, diced

Place a paper towel on bottom of microwave oven. Place potatoes on paper towel. Microwave on 100% power (HIGH) 4 minutes. Turn potatoes over. Microwave on 100% power (HIGH) 3 to 5 minutes more or until just soft when squeezed. Cool; cut in 1/2 lengthwise. Hollow out each potato half, leaving a 1/4-inch-thick shell (reserve potato flesh for other uses). Set shells aside. In a 6-ounce custard cup, microwave margarine on 100% power (HIGH) 45 to 50 seconds or until melted. Stir in dill weed and hot pepper sauce. Brush mixture over both sides of potato skins. Arrange potato skins in a circle, cut-side down, on a microwave-safe plate. Microwave on 100% power (HIGH) 7 to 8 minutes. Turn potato skins over. Sprinkle with cheese and green onions. Adjust power level to 70% power (MEDIUM-HIGH). Microwave 1 minute or until cheese is melted. Makes 6 appetizers.

Carbohydrate 17.3 g	
Protein 6.1 g	
Fat 5.3 g	

Ranch Deviled Eggs

Perfect as a lunchtime side dish or as an appetizer.

4 eggs
2 tablespoons low-fat ranch-type salad
  dressing

1 tablespoon Dijon-style mustard
Paprika to taste
Small fresh parsley sprigs

To hard-cook eggs, wrap each egg in foil. Set aside. In a 4-cup glass measure, microwave 2-1/4 cups water on 100% power (HIGH) 5 minutes. Drop foil-wrapped eggs into water. Microwave on 100% power (HIGH) 10 minutes. Let eggs stand in water 5 minutes. Remove; cool under cold running water. Unwrap eggs; remove shells. Cut each egg in 1/2 lengthwise. Spoon yolks into a small bowl; mash well. Stir in salad dressing and mustard. Pipe or spoon yolk mixture into egg whites. Sprinkle with paprika. Garnish with parsley sprigs. Makes 8 appetizers.

Carbohydrate 1.6 g	
Protein 3.4 g	
Fat 3.7 g	

Clockwise from top: Delicious Almond-Cheese Ball with assorted fresh vegetables, page 144; Marinated Veggies, page 141; Ranch Deviled Eggs

Delicious Almond-Cheese Ball

39 Calories/tablespoon

This cheese ball makes a wonderful holiday gift. Photo on page 143.

1/2 cup sliced almonds (2-1/2 oz.)
1 (8-oz.) package Neufchâtel cheese
1 (6-3/4-oz.) can chunk chicken,
   drained
3 tablespoons chopped green bell pepper

3 tablespoons chopped fresh parsley
2 teaspoons chopped pimento, drained
1/8 teaspoon liquid hickory smoke
Assorted fresh vegetables or
   saltine crackers

In a small microwave-safe bowl, microwave almonds on 100% power (HIGH) 2 to 4 minutes or until brown and toasted, stirring several times during cooking. Set aside. Adjust power to 30% power (MEDIUM-LOW). In a medium microwave-safe bowl, microwave cheese 1-1/2 minutes or until softened. Stir in chicken, bell pepper, parsley, pimento and liquid hickory smoke. Cover tightly. Refrigerate until firm. On a sheet of wax paper, roll cheese mixture into a ball. Roll ball in toasted almonds to coat. Serve with vegetables or crackers. Makes 2-1/4 cups.

Carbohydrate 0.6 g	
Protein 2.2 g	
Fat 3.1 g	

Clam Dip

54 Calories/tablespoon

A low-calorie version of an old favorite.

1/2 (8-oz.) package Neufchâtel cheese
1 (6-1/2-oz.) can minced clams,
   drained
1/3 cup plain low-fat yogurt

1/4 cup diced green onions
1/2 teaspoon Dijon-style mustard
1 teaspoon Worcestershire sauce
Assorted hot cooked or chilled
   raw vegetables

In a medium microwave-safe bowl, microwave cheese on 30% power (MEDIUM-LOW) 1 minute or until softened. Stir in clams, yogurt, onions, mustard and Worcestershire. Adjust power level to 50% power (MEDIUM). Microwave 1 minute. Stir; microwave on 50% power (MEDIUM) 1 to 3 minutes more or until heated through. Serve with hot or cold vegetables. Makes 1-1/4 cups.

Carbohydrate 2.6 g	
Protein 6.2 g	
Fat 1.9 g	

Egg Foo Yung

This versatile dish is good for lunch or dinner. Or, cut in smaller wedges and serve as an appetizer.

**1 (6-oz.) package frozen cooked
  shrimp**
2 teaspoons margarine
4 eggs, beaten
**2-1/2 ounces fresh bean sprouts
  rinsed, drained (1 cup)**

3/4 cup diced green onions
1 garlic clove, minced
1/4 teaspoon black pepper

Foo Yung Sauce:
1 tablespoon cornstarch
3/4 cup water
2 teaspoons lite soy sauce

1 teaspoon chicken-bouillon granules
1/8 teaspoon ground ginger

Remove shrimp from package. Place in a microwave-safe bowl. Microwave on 30% power (MEDIUM-LOW) 2 minutes. Drain; set aside. In a 9-inch microwave-safe pie plate, microwave margarine on 100% power (HIGH) 35 to 40 seconds or until melted. Swirl to coat plate. Set aside. In a medium bowl, combine eggs, shrimp, bean sprouts, green onions, garlic and pepper. Pour into pie plate. Microwave on 100% power (HIGH) 3 minutes. Push cooked outside section of eggs toward center allowing uncooked portion to flow underneath. Adjust power level to 50% power (MEDIUM). Microwave 5 to 6 minutes until set but still moist. Prepare Foo Yung Sauce. Cut eggs in wedges. Serve with sauce. Makes 4 servings.

Foo Yung Sauce:

In a 2-cup glass measure, dissolve cornstarch in water. Stir in soy sauce, bouillon granules and ginger. Microwave on 100% power (HIGH) 1-1/2 to 2 minutes or until thickened, stirring several times during cooking.

Carbohydrate 5.4 g	
Protein 14 g	
Fat 4.4 g	

Mandarin Turkey Meatballs

320 Calories

Mandarin oranges and snow peas give this party dish its bright colors.

1 pound ground turkey
1 egg, lightly beaten
1/2 cup minced onion
1 clove garlic, minced
2 tablespoons grated carrot
3 tablespoons lite soy sauce
Water
1-1/2 teaspoons cornstarch

1/2 teaspoon ground ginger
8 ounces fresh snow peas, ends
   and strings removed
1 teaspoon water
1 (11-oz.) can mandarin orange sections,
   drained
3 cups hot, cooked rice

In a large bowl, thoroughly mix turkey, egg, onion, garlic, carrot and 1 tablespoon of soy sauce. Shape in 1-inch balls. Arrange meatballs in a circle in a shallow microwave-safe dish or pie plate. Microwave on 100% power (HIGH) 3 minutes. Rearrange, moving outside meatballs to center of dish. Microwave on 100% power (HIGH) 2 to 3 minutes more or until no longer pink in center (cut to test). Transfer meatballs to a large serving bowl; set aside. Drain juice into a 4-cup glass measure. Add enough water to make 3/4 cup liquid. Dissolve cornstarch in liquid. Stir in remaining 2 tablespoons of soy sauce and ginger. Microwave on 100% power (HIGH) 2 to 3 minutes or until sauce is clear and slightly thickened, stirring every minute during cooking. Set aside. Place snow peas in a small microwave-safe bowl. Sprinkle with 1 teaspoon water. Cover tightly. Microwave on 100% power (HIGH) 2 minutes. Stir snow peas into meatballs. Pour sauce over all. Carefully stir in mandarin orange sections. Serve over rice. Makes 6 servings.

Carbohydrate 37.5 g	
Protein 31.1 g	
Fat 4.6 g	

Bean & Corn Bake

160 Calories

Vegetable proteins team up in this great dish.

3/4 cup chopped onion
1 small green bell pepper, seeded,
  cut in strips
1/2 cup sliced celery
2 cloves garlic, minced
1 (16-oz.) can tomatoes
1 tablespoon Worcestershire sauce
1-1/2 teaspoons Italian herb seasoning

1 (17-oz.) can whole kernel corn,
  drained, rinsed
1 (15-oz.) can kidney beans,
  drained, rinsed
1 (15-oz.) can pinto beans,
  drained, rinsed
2/3 cup shredded part-skim
  mozzarella cheese (2-2/3 oz.)

In a 2-1/2-quart microwave-safe casserole dish, combine onion, bell pepper, celery and garlic. Cover tightly. Microwave on 100% power (HIGH) 2-1/2 minutes. Stir in tomatoes with juice, Worcestershire sauce, herb seasoning, corn, kidney beans and pinto beans; recover. Microwave on 100% power (HIGH) 10 minutes or until heated through, stirring several times during cooking. Sprinkle with cheese. Makes 10 servings.

Carbohydrate 27.5 g	
Protein 9.7 g	
Fat 2.4 g	

Oven-Browned Potatoes

171 Calories

One medium potato has only about 90 calories.

1 tablespoon margarine
1/2 teaspoon browning sauce
1/4 teaspoon dried leaf herb of
  your choice

1/4 teaspoon paprika
4 small (3-1/2 oz.) baking potatoes, peeled,
  cut in quarters

In a shallow 1-1/2-quart microwave-safe casserole dish, microwave margarine on 100% power (HIGH) 45 to 50 seconds or until melted. Stir in browning sauce, herb and paprika. Add potatoes; turn to coat with margarine mixture. Microwave on 100% power (HIGH) 6 to 8 minutes or until fork-tender, stirring several times during cooking. Makes 4 servings.

Carbohydrate 32.8 g	
Protein 4 g	
Fat 3.1 g	

Pasta Primavera

300 Calories

A bright dish loaded with fresh vegetables. Perfect for a luncheon.

1-1/4 cups uncooked pasta spirals
1 cup fresh broccoli flowerets
1 carrot, thinly sliced
1/2 cup asparagus, cut in
   1-inch pieces
1/2 cup sliced zucchini or
   crookneck squash
1/4 cup coarsely chopped red or green
   bell pepper

1/4 cup margarine
2 tablespoons dry white wine
1/3 cup evaporated milk
1/2 cup grated Parmesan cheese
   (1-1/2 oz.)
1/2 teaspoon dried leaf thyme
1/4 teaspoon dried leaf tarragon

In an 8-cup glass measure, microwave 2-1/2 cups water on 100% power (HIGH) 8 minutes or until boiling. Add pasta. Microwave on 100% power (HIGH) 5 to 6 minutes or until tender. Drain; set aside. In a 2-quart microwave-safe casserole dish, combine broccoli, carrot, asparagus, squash, bell pepper and 1 tablespoon of margarine. Cover tightly. Microwave on 100% power (HIGH) 4 to 5 minutes or until carrot is almost tender. Mix in pasta; set aside. In a 2-cup glass measure, combine remaining 3 tablespoons of margarine, wine, milk, cheese, thyme and tarragon. Microwave on 100% power (HIGH) 1 to 2 minutes or until heated through, stirring every 30 seconds during cooking. Pour over pasta mixture; toss lightly. Makes 4 servings.

Carbohydrate 33.5 g	
Protein 13.0 g	
Fat 11.2 g	

Marvelous Mushrooms

41 Calories

Great as an appetizer or a side dish. Photo on page 4.

8 ounces fresh mushrooms
1 tablespoon white distilled vinegar
1/4 cup diced green onions
2 tablespoons diced red bell pepper
1 tablespoon lemon juice

1 teaspoon sugar
1/4 teaspoon dried leaf thyme
1/3 cup dairy sour cream
2 tablespoons chopped fresh parsley

Place mushrooms in a 1-quart microwave-safe casserole dish. Carefully stir in vinegar, green onions and bell pepper. Cover tightly. Microwave on 100% power (HIGH) 2 minutes. Drain; cool. In a 1-cup glass measure, combine lemon juice, sugar, thyme and sour cream. Pour over mushrooms; mix well. Cover tightly. Refrigerate several hours. To serve, sprinkle with parsley. Makes 6 servings.

Carbohydrate 3.3 g	
Protein 1.3 g	
Fat 2.7 g	

Canadian Asparagus Muffins

218 Calories

Curry powder gives the sauce a special flavor.

1-1/2 pounds fresh asparagus, washed
3 tablespoons water
1 (10-3/4-oz.) can cream of mushroom soup
1/4 cup skim milk
6 ounces fresh mushrooms, sliced (2 cups)
1/2 teaspoon onion powder

1/2 teaspoon curry powder
4 hard-cooked eggs, chopped
4 English muffins, split, toasted
8 Canadian bacon slices
Small fresh parsley sprigs

Snap off and discard tough stalk ends of asparagus. Arrange spears, buds toward center, in a shallow microwave-safe dish. Add water. Cover tightly. Microwave on 100% power (HIGH) 3 minutes. Rearrange, moving outside spears to center of dish; recover. Microwave on 100% power (HIGH) 3 to 5 minutes more or until almost tender. Let stand 5 minutes. In a 4-cup glass measure, combine soup, milk, mushrooms, onion powder and curry powder. Microwave on 100% power (HIGH) 2 to 3 minutes. Stir in eggs. Arrange muffin halves, cut-side up in a circle, on a large microwave-safe plate. Top each muffin half with 1 Canadian bacon slice. Drain asparagus. Place spears on Canadian bacon slices. Spoon soup mixture over top. Adjust power level to 70% power (MEDIUM-HIGH). Microwave 2 minutes or until heated through. Garnish with parsley sprigs. Makes 8 servings.

Carbohydrate 22 g	
Protein 14.2 g	
Fat 9 g	

Marinated Potato Salad

94 Calories

The old-fashioned flavor of German potato salad with the ease of microwave cooking.

1 pound red thin-skinned potatoes,
    scrubbed, cut in 1/2-inch cubes
1 tablespoon water
1 celery stalk, diagonally sliced
1 small red onion, thinly sliced

1/2 cup diced green bell pepper
Dash black pepper
1/3 cup oil-free Italian salad dressing
Small fresh parsley sprigs

Place potatoes in a 1-1/2-quart microwave-safe casserole dish. Sprinkle with water. Cover tightly. Microwave on 100% power (HIGH) 3 minutes. Stir; recover. Microwave on 100% power (HIGH) 3 to 4 minutes more or until fork-tender. Cool. Mix in celery, onion, bell pepper and black pepper. Stir in salad dressing. Cover tightly. Refrigerate several hours or overnight. Toss gently before serving. Garnish with parsley sprigs. Makes 6 servings.

Carbohydrate 15.2 g	
Protein 2 g	
Fat 3.1 g	

Curried Fruit

Curried fruit makes a wonderful side dish with ham or pork.

**1 (8-oz.) can chunk pineapple packed
  in unsweetened pineapple juice**
**1 (16-oz.) can apricot halves packed
  in juice**
**1 (16-oz.) can pear halves packed
  in juice**

1 teaspoon cornstarch
1 tablespoon packed brown sugar
1/2 teaspoon curry powder
1/4 teaspoon ground cinnamon

Drain pineapple, apricots and pears. Combine juices; reserve 3/4 cup. Layer pineapple, apricots and pears in a shallow 2-quart microwave-safe casserole dish. Set aside. In a 2-cup glass measure, combine reserved 3/4 cup fruit juices, cornstarch, brown sugar, curry powder and cinnamon. Stir until cornstarch and sugar dissolve. Microwave on 100% power (HIGH) 2 to 3 minutes or until clear and slightly thickened, stirring every minute during cooking. Pour over fruit. Adjust power level to 70% power (MEDIUM-HIGH). Microwave 4 to 5 minutes or until heated through. Makes 6 servings.

Carbohydrate 41 g	
Protein 0.7 g	
Fat 0.3 g	

Zucchini Parmesan

A simple, savory way to fix a favorite summer vegetable.

**1 pound zucchini, cut in
  1/4-inch-thick slices**
1/2 teaspoon dried leaf oregano

1/4 teaspoon butter-flavored salt
2 tablespoons grated Parmesan cheese

Spread zucchini in a 1-1/2-quart microwave-safe casserole dish. Sprinkle with oregano. Cover tightly. Microwave on 100% power (HIGH) 3 minutes. Stir; recover. Microwave on 100% power (HIGH) 2 to 3 minutes more or until zucchini is tender. Sprinkle with butter-flavored salt and cheese. Makes 6 servings.

Carbohydrate 2.6 g	
Protein 2.3 g	
Fat 1.3 g	

Fruit-Topped Custard

171 Calories

A simple, calcium-rich dessert.

3 eggs
1/4 cup sugar
1 teaspoon vanilla extract
1/4 teaspoon salt
1-1/2 cups skim milk

Ground nutmeg to taste
1 cup sliced fresh strawberries
1/2 cup fresh blueberries
Fresh mint sprigs, if desired

In a medium bowl, beat eggs, sugar, vanilla and salt. Set aside. In a 4-cup glass measure, microwave milk on 100% power (HIGH) 3-1/2 minutes or until scalded. Gradually add milk to egg mixture, stirring constantly. Pour into 4 (6-oz.) dessert dishes or custard cups. Arrange in a circle in microwave oven. Adjust power level to 30% power (MEDIUM-LOW). Microwave 10 to 13 minutes or until a knife inserted just off center comes out clean, rearranging every 3 minutes during cooking. As each custard is done, remove to a wire rack; cool. Cover tightly; refrigerate. Serve in dessert dishes. Or, carefully unmold by running a spatula around edges and inverting on individual dessert plates. Sprinkle with nutmeg. Top with strawberries and blueberries. Garnish with mint sprigs, if desired. Makes 4 servings.

Carbohydrate 23.5 g	
Protein 8.4 g	
Fat 5.3 g	

Rich Chocolate Ice Cream

97 Calories

Super-rich chocolate flavor with half the fat calories.

1 (12-oz.) can evaporated skim milk
1/3 cup unsweetened cocoa powder
1/4 cup sugar

1/8 teaspoon ground cinnamon
14 large marshmallows

Pour 1 cup of milk into a 4-cup glass measure. Refrigerate until chilled. Refrigerate beaters of an electric mixer until cold. In a medium microwave-safe bowl, combine cocoa, sugar and cinnamon. Stir in remaining milk. Add marshmallows. Microwave on 50% power (MEDIUM) 2 to 3 minutes or until marshmallows are melted, stirring every minute during cooking. Cool. Beat chilled milk with chilled beaters until stiff. Fold into cooled cocoa mixture. Pour into a 2-quart casserole dish. Cover tightly. Freeze until firm. Makes 10 (about 1/2-cup) servings.

Carbohydrate 19.9 g	
Protein 4.1 g	
Fat 0.5 g	

Fruit Pizza

This makes a perfect party dessert.

1 cup all-purpose flour
1/4 cup cornstarch
1/4 cup sugar
1/3 cup firm margarine
1 egg, beaten
1 (8-oz.) package Neufchâtel cheese

3 tablespoons sugar
1/2 teaspoon almond flavoring
2 cups assorted fresh fruit
(strawberries, sliced kiwifruit,
seedless green grapes or sliced
nectarines)

Coat a round 10-inch glass pizza plate with cooking spray. In a medium bowl, combine flour, cornstarch and 1/4 cup sugar. Using a pastry blender or 2 knives, cut in margarine until mixture is crumbly. Mix in egg. Shape dough in a ball; place in prepared pizza plate. Press to cover bottom evenly. Microwave on 100% power (HIGH) 4 to 5 minutes or until center of crust is set. Cool. Adjust power level to 30% power (MEDIUM-LOW). In a small microwave-safe bowl, microwave cheese 1-1/2 minutes or until softened. Beat in 3 tablespoons sugar and almond extract until smooth. Spread over crust; refrigerate until cold. To serve, arrange fruit attractively atop cheese mixture. Makes 10 servings.

Carbohydrate 25 g	
Protein 4.3 g	
Fat 11.6 g	

How to Make Fruit Pizza

1/Softened cheese mixture is evenly spread over pre-baked "pizza" crust. Both can be prepared ahead and refrigerated.

2/Just before serving, pizza is decorated with assorted fresh fruit, attractively arranged atop filling.

Peach Fondue

62 Calories without fresh-fruit dippers

A refreshing finale to any meal. Spear fruit on forks to dip. Photo on page 4.

1 (16-oz.) can peach halves packed
  in water
1-1/2 teaspoons cornstarch
1/4 teaspoon ground cinnamon

1/8 teaspoon ground allspice
1-1/2 tablespoons sugar
1/2 teaspoon vanilla extract
Assorted fresh fruit

In a food processor fitted with a metal blade or in a blender, combine peaches with juice, cornstarch, cinnamon, allspice and sugar. Process until smooth. Pour into a 4-cup glass measure. Microwave on 100% power (HIGH) 4 to 5 minutes or until clear and thickened, stirring every minute during cooking. Stir in vanilla. Keep fondue warm in a fondue pot or chafing dish with a candle. Serve with fruit for dipping. Makes 8 (1/4 cup) servings.

Carbohydrate 15.8 g	
Protein 0.3 g	
Fat 0.1 g	

Raspberry-Mandarin Sauce

13 Calories/tablespoon

Great over ice milk or angel food cake.

1 (11-oz.) can mandarin orange sections
1/4 cup low-sugar red raspberry spread
1 tablespoon lemon juice

2 teaspoons cornstarch
1/8 teaspoon ground nutmeg
Few drops red food coloring, if desired

Drain mandarin orange sections, reserving 1/4 cup juice. Set mandarin orange sections aside. In a 4-cup glass measure, combine reserved juice, raspberry spread, lemon juice, cornstarch and nutmeg. Microwave on 100% power (HIGH) 1 to 2 minutes or until thickened, stirring every minute during cooking. Stir in mandarin orange sections and food coloring, if desired. Serve hot. Or, cool, cover tightly and refrigerate. Makes 1 cup sauce.

Carbohydrate 3.5 g	
Protein 0.1 g	
Fat 0 g	

Cherries Jubilee

159 Calories

The alcohol in the cherry brandy evaporates when heated—taking calories away with it!

1 (16-oz.) package frozen unsweetened
  pitted dark sweet cherries
1 tablespoon cornstarch

1/3 cup low-sugar grape spread
1/4 cup cherry brandy
1-1/2 pints vanilla ice milk

Using a fork, puncture 1 end of cherry bag. Set bag in a microwave-safe bowl. Microwave on 100% power (HIGH) 3-1/2 minutes. Drain cherries 5 minutes in a strainer set over a 2-quart microwave-safe casserole dish. Set cherries aside. Dissolve cornstarch in cherry juice. Stir in grape spread. Microwave on 100% power (HIGH) 2 to 2-1/2 minutes or until clear and thickened, stirring several times during cooking. Stir in cherries. Microwave on 100% power (HIGH) 3 minutes or until cherries are heated through. In a 1-cup glass measure, microwave cherry brandy on 100% power (HIGH) 25 seconds. Pour over hot cherry mixture; carefully ignite. Stir, spooning sauce over cherries, until flames subside. Place 1/2 cup ice milk in 6 dessert dishes. Spoon hot cherries over each. Makes 6 servings.

Carbohydrate 31.2 g	
Protein 3.3 g	
Fat 3.1 g	

Easy Peach Cobbler

214 Calories

Makes a perfect summer dessert after a light meal.

3 peaches, peeled, pitted, sliced
3/4 cup baking mix
3 tablespoons sugar
1/2 teaspoon almond extract

1/4 cup skim milk
1 teaspoon margarine
1 teaspoon ground cinnamon
1/4 cup chopped walnuts

Arrange peaches evenly over bottom of a round 8-inch microwave-safe dish. In a small bowl, combine baking mix, 2 tablespoons of sugar, almond extract and milk. Drop batter evenly by teaspoonful over peaches. Dot with margarine. In a custard cup, combine remaining 1 tablespoon of sugar, cinnamon and walnuts. Sprinkle over batter. Microwave on 100% power (HIGH) 5 to 6 minutes or until batter topping is set. Serve warm. Makes 4 servings.

Carbohydrate 30.2 g	
Protein 6.6 g	
Fat 8.4 g	

Chocolate Sauce

23 Calories/tablespoon

A great sauce for the health-conscious chocoholic. Calories are reduced by more than half.

2 teaspoons cornstarch
1/4 cup unsweetened cocoa powder
1/3 cup sugar

1/2 cup water
1 teaspoon vanilla extract

In a 2-cup glass measure, combine cornstarch, cocoa and sugar. Stir in water and vanilla until smooth. Microwave on 100% power (HIGH) 1 to 2 minutes or until thickened, stirring once or twice during cooking. Serve hot. Or, cool, cover tightly and refrigerate. Makes 1 cup.

Carbohydrate 4.9 g	
Protein 0.4 g	
Fat 0.2 g	

Metric Chart

Comparison to Metric Measure

When You Know	Symbol	Multiply By	To Find	Symbol
teaspoons	tsp	5.0	milliliters	ml
tablespoons	tbsp	15.0	milliliters	ml
fluid ounces	fl. oz.	30.0	milliliters	ml
cups	c	0.24	liters	l
pints	pt.	0.47	liters	l

When You Know	Symbol	Multiply By	To Find	Symbol
quarts	qt.	0.95	liters	l
ounces	oz.	28.0	grams	g
pounds	lb.	0.45	kilograms	kg
Fahrenheit	F	5/9 (after subtracting 32)	Celsius	C

Liquid Measure to Liters

1/4 cup	=	0.06 liters
1/2 cup	=	0.12 liters
3/4 cup	=	0.18 liters
1 cup	=	0.24 liters
1-1/4 cups	=	0.3 liters
1-1/2 cups	=	0.36 liters
2 cups	=	0.48 liters
2-1/2 cups	=	0.6 liters
3 cups	=	0.72 liters
3-1/2 cups	=	0.84 liters
4 cups	=	0.96 liters
4-1/2 cups	=	1.08 liters
5 cups	=	1.2 liters
5-1/2 cups	=	1.32 liters

Liquid Measure to Milliliters

1/4 teaspoon	=	1.25 milliliters
1/2 teaspoon	=	2.5 milliliters
3/4 teaspoon	=	3.75 milliliters
1 teaspoon	=	5.0 milliliters
1-1/4 teaspoons	=	6.25 milliliters
1-1/2 teaspoons	=	7.5 milliliters
1-3/4 teaspoons	=	8.75 milliliters
2 teaspoons	=	10.0 milliliters
1 tablespoon	=	15.0 milliliters
2 tablespoons	=	30.0 milliliters

Fahrenheit to Celsius

F	C
200—205	95
220—225	105
245—250	120
275	135
300—305	150
325—330	165
345—350	175
370—375	190
400—405	205
425—430	220
445—450	230
470—475	245
500	260

POWER LEVEL SETTINGS

Word Designation	Numerical Designation	Power Output at Setting	Percentage of HIGH Setting
HIGH	10	650 watts	100%
MEDIUM HIGH	7	455 watts	70%
MEDIUM	5	325 watts	50%
MEDIUM LOW	3	195 watts	30%
LOW	1	65 watts	10%

Index